THE GOLDEN LYRE

Plays and Satires

THE GOLDEN LYRE

Plays and Satires

Revised Edition

L. J. Fattorosi

With Illustrations by
Robert R. Brown

VIMINAL BOOKS
Lakewood, New Jersey

Published by: Viminal Books
          20 Genesee Place
          Lakewood, N.J. 08701

Library of Congress Catalog Card Number: 96-61631

The Tragedy of The Golden Lyre is based on "Orpheus," a dramatic poem that appeared in *Orpheus and Other Poems*, Pageant Press, © 1958 by Louis J. Fattorosi.

"Science; a Recasting of Shelley's 'Ozymandias'" and "The Death of Patroclus" appeared in slightly different form in *Orpheus and Other Poems*.

"Satire V" from *The Scourge of Vacuity* appeared in slightly different form in *The National Review,* 2 June 1970.

Printed in the United States of America
on acid free paper.

ISBN 0-9655135-0-5

To Karen

CONTENTS

ILLUSTRATIONS

ACKNOWLEDGMENTS

I wish to express my gratitude and acknowledge my indebtedness first to my friend and mentor, Aubrey Williams, Professor Emeritus, University of Florida, for his close and critical reading of the manuscript of *The Golden Lyre* and *Prometheus Unvanquished* and for indicating inconsistencies and lapses. I am also much indebted to another friend and mentor, Donald J. McGinn, Professor Emeritus, Rutgers University and Georgian Court College, especially for his criticism of the preface to *The Golden Lyre*.

I have also received helpful criticism from University of Florida professors Alastair Duckworth and Richard Brantley, from Poet Laureate Richard Wilbur, Professor Emeritus, Harvard University, from my friends June Clayton, Norman Slade, and A. Kevin Quinn, and from my wife, Karen. For inaugurating the business attendant upon publishing, I am grateful for the help of my friend Lawrence Terzian and for the guidance and patience of my production manager, Arthur Hamparian.

L. J. Fattorosi

PART I

The Golden Lyre

Prometheus Unvanquished

Shorter Poems

The Golden Lyre

A Tragedy in Three Acts

To his music, plants and flowers
Ever sprung; as sun and showers
There had made a lasting spring.

—Shakespeare

PREFACE

I

In *The Golden Lyre,* as in *Prometheus Unvanquished,* it has been my intention to contribute to a familiar but complex myth by drawing upon universal themes of Classical literature and by employing the flexible idiom of the Renaissance, the classic diction of English poetry. Suiting the style to the matter, I have attempted to reflect the cadences and the diction of English verse from Spenser to Arnold. The theme common to both plays is man's inordinate ambition and the paradox of his godlike nobility at his best and his human imperfection even at his best. In the first play the theme is articulated by Orpheus; in the second it is implicit in the quarrel between Zeus and Prometheus. Earlier versions of both plays have been successfully produced on the amateur stage.

The Golden Lyre is based on the myth of Orpheus and Eurydice, the earliest extant sources of which are Vergil's *Georgics* IV and Ovid's *Metamorphoses* X. Boethius retold the myth in *The Consolation of Philosophy* III. The only English version is Robert Henryson's *Orpheus and Eurydice,* a fifteenth century poem.[1] Although the tale is among the most familiar of Classical myths, no serious English version of it in dramatic form exists. Since Politian's *La favola*

---

1. The fourteenth century metrical romance *Sir Orfeo* and the later ballad based on it, "King Orfeo," bear small resemblance to the Classical myth.

5

d'Orfeo (1492), for all its brevity, may be regarded as the first notable secular play of the modern era, and Monteverdi and Striggio's *Orfeo* (1607) the first great opera, it seems remarkable that in all English literature the dramatic possibilities of the renowned tragic tale were not exploited long ago.

I have remained faithful to the outline of the myth, making only those changes I deemed dramatically expedient, but I have not patterned my play on any previous work. Set in the mythic past, the action begins immediately before the wedding of Orpheus and Eurydice. Soon after the nuptial ceremony, the festive mood ends abruptly with the death of Eurydice, who has been stung by a venomous serpent. Through the power of his art, the bereaved lover descends into the underworld, surmounts every peril, and prevails on Hades to restore Eurydice to life. Before completing his journey back to the upper world, however, he turns to look upon his bride and thus violates a condition imposed by the infernal god. As a result Eurydice dies a second death, and Orpheus, overcome with grief and remorse, returns alone to "the world of light and flowers," never to see his bride again. He has conquered Hades only to be vanquished by his own frailty.

The Golden Lyre is the story of man's heroic struggle to transcend the limitations of his own nature. Orpheus is noble, but he is flawed. His intelligence and his art almost make a god of him. His art momentarily enables him to recover his bride from the underworld, but his failure to rule and overcome his passions leads him to a grievous error in judgment and deprives him of his victory. Orpheus is the best of poets, but, having thus erred, all his art is not sufficient to reclaim Eurydice from death. It is doubtful that the art of Orpheus (or the arts of man), no matter how refined or exalted, can surmount his mortality. Underlying the drama is the unresolved question of free will versus fate and divine forethought.

According to one version of the myth, Orpheus is the son of Apollo; according to another he is the son of a mortal, Oeagrus, and the Muse Calliope. I have disregarded any suggestion of his divine or semi-divine origin in order to emphasize his humanity.

The purpose of the two epithalamion scenes beginning the first act is twofold: to suggest a remote and timeless past, which helps establish a poetic distancing between the audience and the play, and to create a festive mood of celebration in contrast to the impending tragedy (Freytag's "inciting moment"). With the commencement of the rising action, pastoral lyricism is gradually abandoned in favor of diction more appropriate to the changing circumstances of the action.

II

I should have preferred to abstain from critical comment; a play should have no need of extraneous matter to recommend it. Nevertheless, considering how academic critics may have prejudiced the minds of serious readers against such traditional forms as I have adopted, I find it expedient to attempt a critical defense—not of my plays, but of those principles upon which they have been composed. That defense constitutes the main part of this preface.

I have thought it best to treat the myth in a traditional manner; contemporary forms, it seems to me, would be inappropriate to my theme. Here the reader will find no fragmented drama, no obscure symbolism, no innovative eccentricities. I have tried to achieve dramatic truth and universality, well aware that according to structuralist criticism they are unattainable. The latest criticism, like the latest art, is not invariably the best. "The literary world," said Somerset Maugham, "lacks balance, and when a fancy takes it, is apt to regard it not as a passing fashion, but as heaven's first law."[2] To pursue an independent course, however, is to court obscurity—at least for the present.

---

2. *The Summing Up* (New York: The Literary Guild of America, 1938), p. 208.

In our universities the free exchange of ideas is a principle more often violated than honored. Aleksandr Solzhenitsyn, in his commencement address delivered at Harvard University on June 8, 1978, thus reproached American academic circles for the establishment of party lines and the collateral suppression of unfashionable "trends of thought":

> Without any censorship in the West, fashionable
> trends of thought and ideas are fastidiously
> separated from those that are not fashionable,
> and the latter, without ever being forbidden, have
> little chance of finding their way into . . . books or
> being heard in colleges. Your scholars are free in
> the legal sense, but they are hemmed in by the
> idols of the prevailing fad.[3]

Jacques Ellul, referring to the decline of the West, speaks out in a similar vein when he charges all contemporary artists and intellectuals with *blind negation,* an unqualified rejection of Western cultural tradition, a dissociation from the past. Now he says *all* because those not in accord with fashionable and doctrinal art forms are ignored and therefore do not count.

According to Ellul, beyond the blind negation of contemporary artists and intellectuals,

> there is nothing—except the void that is their
> work. Fragmented theater . . . poetry without
> words and music that is sheer noise, destructured
> language, Lacan, Derrida . . . who think that
> absolute incomprehensibility offers a way out.[4]

Whether or not Ellul overstates his case, it is not unreasonable to say that the works of contemporary artists frequently lack a measure of sanity and sometimes represent

---

3. *A World Split Apart,* trans. Irina Ilovayskaya Alberti (New York: Harper and Row, 1978), p. 29.
4. *The Betrayal of the West,* trans. Matthew O'Connell (New York: The Seabury Press, 1978), p. 197.

a travesty of art. For most of this century poets have deliberately shunned eloquence and cultivated obscurity by distorting their syntax and wrenching diction loose from the constraints of reason. Unfortunately for them, posterity has a way of forgetting art that is obscure. What is obscure in its own time is in a fair way of becoming incomprehensible to future generations.

"Art for art's sake," a movement that proceeded from nineteenth century aesthetics, contributed much to a radical break in tradition—a break which occurred in the last quarter of the century, spawning new schools of disjunctive art, among them cubism, free-form sculpture, atonal music, and symbolist poetry. The most characteristic avant-garde art of the revolutionary twentieth century imitates nothing in nature, for it is unique. There is nothing in creation quite like it. It has no literary, historical, or philosophical reference. It has, in brief, no *human* reference. It is entirely original and represents or suggests nothing extrinsic to itself. Conversely, the orthodox art of the West is primarily empirical and humanistic: empirical in that it is traditional, representing the accumulated experience of history; humanistic in that it is man-centered. Historically, Western art imitates nature as nature pertains to man. The plays of Shakespeare, like the frescoes of Michelangelo, are imitations of nature heightened and intensified.

III

In a general way I have emulated Classical and Renaissance models, but I have written with my own pen. Having recourse to conventions need not diminish a writer's creativity; on the contrary, it may enhance it. Among modernists it is a common opinion that anything familiar or derivative (disparaging terms in their usage) cannot possibly be fresh or original. T. S. Eliot challenged that assumption:

> We shall often find that not only the best but the
> most individual parts of . . . a poet's work may be
> those in which the dead poets, his ancestors,
> assert their immortality most vigorously.[5]

In a real sense the literature of the past is alive and present
in the literature of our time when it manifests itself in
allusions and in conventions of style, structure, and often
content. With characteristic lucidity and grace Sir Joshua
Reynolds in his "Sixth Presidential Discourse," delivered
at the Royal Academy (1774), had this to say:

> The greatest natural genius cannot subsist on his
> own stock: he who resolves never to ransack any
> mind but his own, will soon be reduced, from
> mere barrenness, to the poorest of all imitations;
> he will be obliged to imitate himself, and to
> repeat what he has often repeated.[6]

It would be difficult to think of a major poet, besides
Homer and Aeschylus, whose work could not be called
derivative—and we know next to nothing about the
antecedents of Homer and Aeschylus.

Critics will occasionally confuse originality with eccentricity. Originality of no great consequence lies in the use
of eccentric diction or in the mere invention of new plots.
Sir Henry Newbolt expatiates on this theme:

> The more a writer struggles to invent the less he
> is likely to create. His true way is a different one;
> he finds his material among the accumulated
> stories of the race, whether ancient or modern;
> he sets to work to reject all that he judges
> unnecessary or unfit, to add all that is lacking;
> and finally . . . he endows his work with his own

---

5. "Tradition and the Individual Talent," *Selected Essays* (New
York: Harcourt, Brace, 1932), p. 4.
6. *Discourses on Art,* ed. Robert R. Wark (San Marino, California:
Huntington Library, 1959), p. 99.

personal quality in the act of making it serve his own purpose.[7]

Goethe believed that Renaissance poets achieved greatness when they discovered a potent truth of the ancients: that poets may claim as their own preserve all of literature and not be timorous of saying something simply because it might have been said before. They prized not novelty, but mastery (the phrase is Gore Vidal's).

The history of literature presents convincing evidence that convention and spontaneity are indeed compatible. In *Art and Illusion* E. H. Gombrich notes that Romanticism "was interested only in what was new and original" (i.e., original in the narrow sense). But he adds, "The very existence of styles and traditions has made us doubtful of the value of this approach to the history of art."[8] Brian Vickers concurs with Gombrich:

> It is a paradox that . . . it was only by
> subordinating himself to the conventions of art
> that a writer could . . . express his personal vision
> of a coherent, objective form. But it is a paradox
> which did not disturb Shakespeare. It disturbs
> only those who regard "conventions" as being
> inimical to creativity.[9]

In 1860 Matthew Arnold's *Sohrab and Rustum* appeared, "a wonderfully stately epic," said Oscar Wilde, "full of the spirit of Homer." He might well have added that it has much of Homer's manner. In observing the epic conventions, Arnold employs the traditional English heroic idiom: classic diction in blank verse. More than twenty-five centuries separate *Sohrab and Rustum* from the

---

7. Quoted in A. F. Scott, *The Poet's Craft* (1957; rpt. New York: Dover, 1967), p. x.
8. Quoted by Brian Vickers, *Classical Rhetoric in English Poetry* (Edinburgh: Macmillan, 1970), p. 78.
9. Vickers, p. 78.

Iliad; yet the epic conventions are similarly observed in both poems—even to the extent that several of Arnold's epic similes could be substituted for several of Homer's, *mutatis mutandis,* without doing violence to Homer's poem. A close reading of Arnold's poem should demonstrate, as it probably did to Wilde, that Arnold patterned much of his style on Homer's masterpiece and that Arnold's poem is the better for his having done so. It may therefore be said that his poem is derivative and that it is the better for being derivative; moreover, a similar case can be made for the derivative character of such works as the *Aeneid, Troilus and Criseyde, The Faerie Queene,* and *Hamlet.*

Arnold's use of *imitatio* reflects the commonly accepted practice of poets from Hellenistic times through most of the eighteenth century, a practice recommended by Horace, Quintilian, and Longinus. *Imitatio,* not to be confused with mere copying, is best defined as emulation of the spirit and manner of the masters. A synthesis of *imitatio* and Aristotelian *mimesis* (i.e., imitation of human actions and, more broadly, of *nature*) was suggested by Vida and the elder Scaliger in the sixteenth century and formalized in the seventeenth by Boileau, who believed that the truest way to imitate nature is to emulate the masters. Pope expressed this neo-classic synthesis in *An Essay on Criticism,* in which he imagined Vergil scorning to draw upon any other source or model but nature, only to find that *"Nature* and *Homer* were the *same."* Although as early as the last two or three decades of the eighteenth century *imitatio* fell into disfavor among romanticists who pursued originality of a more innovative kind, poets from Keats to Eliot continued to avail themselves of the method. In practice, if not in precept, Wordsworth himself did not cavil at emulating the masters even as he competed with them.

Horace contended that if an artist had sufficient talent or genius, his emulation would produce new and original art. Through the medium of the artist the old models are transformed. Goethe thought that too many poets of his own time wasted creative energy on the wrong kind of originality, originality of an inconsequential kind—"mere singularity," Berenson called it. These were the romanticist poets who sought above all else to do something that had never been done before. To what extent it was worth doing or whether it was worth doing at all are questions they seldom bothered to ask themselves. Goethe's characterization of them may with even greater justice be applied to many modernist and post-modernist poets: "They crawl into dark corners and carve upon nutshells." Theirs is a coterie art of curious metaphors and small scope.

IV

It is not uncommon to find among critics of this century and the last those who speak of poetry as if the only true poems were lyrics, brief and intimately private expressions of strong emotions, as if all that poetry had to offer were the "intense moment" that is pressed like a rose between the pages of an old tome—the scent of its petals miraculously preserved for another time. Thus all poetry must be brief; for in this view, as Poe had it, a long poem is either impossible or it consists of a series of intense moments (or short poems) set in a framework of metrical prose. In other words all genuine poems are lyrics, and poems that are not lyrics are not poems at all, but merely prose in verse form—save for the occasional lyric passage that crops up *passim*. I find this view of poetry narrow, sentimental, and altogether unconvincing. Though a long narrative poem or a verse drama may have intense moments, which may or may *not* be lyrical, they can only be incidental to the composition as a whole, unless the composition is an instrument designed for the display of intense moments, in which circumstance the unity of the work may well be impaired or even sacrificed.

Shorter verse forms like the ballad, the sonnet, and brief lyrics of a less formal or disciplined character are surely as capable of great beauty as are major forms like the epic and verse tragedy. They differ chiefly in scale or scope. The mannered verse that has dominated and sometimes diminished twentieth century poetry, however, is verse of another order. Its limitations may be seen especially in the lyric forms in which imagery, symbolism, and the disjunctive phrase become the poem's raison d'etre. In motion pictures that might have been designed to please avant-garde cinema aestheticians, a similar emphasis may be discerned: in these it is the cinematic technique—the frenetic quick-cuts, the composition in the frame, the glint of sunlight on the camera lens, and the special effects— that supersedes the plot, the dialogue, and the theme, all of which are relegated to mere opportunities for clever photography. The frantic search for innovative techniques seems to have produced much of the fragmented art of recent years, the mannered art in which the means become the end: the kind of art-in-little that Goethe regarded as nutshell carving.

For the last two centuries art has been widely perceived as self-expression, an attitude which Matthew Arnold considered as engendering caprice and eccentricity. That it can also engender self-indulgence is not surprising. He thought that poetry is best served when the poet regards not himself but his work and when he sees his work steadily and sees it whole. When a poet makes himself the subject of a poem, he is prone to fall into the particular and the trivial, and his task becomes self-limiting. In his preface to the 1854 edition of *Poems,* where he speaks of poems containing an action (e.g., verse drama and dramatic and narrative poems), Arnold suggests that it is the poet's self-expression which misdirects him to expend his powers on phrases and images and pay scant attention to the action and to the work as a whole. Not only does the modern critic permit this false practice, he writes, but "he absolutely prescribes false aims." Arnold regarded style as a function of the action and not as a reflection of the poet's personality.

In dramatic verse, surely, the best style is that which is best suited to the characters and to the action generated by them: the action of the play as a whole and of the parts that are integrated into the unity of the whole. The beauties of imagery and diction shine more brightly when they rise from the exigencies of the action, when style and content are harmoniously bound together.

I have employed a rhetorical style, usually of direct statement, because I think it appropriate to the genre and the action. Modernist poets may think it more artistic to perplex than please, but the style of the imagist or the symbolist, however successfully it may be managed in lyrics, is demonstrably ill-suited to dramatic verse. It more becomes the study than the stage. Dramatic verse demands immediate intelligibility if it is to seize the attention and sustain the interest of an audience. Furthermore, an effective way of losing an audience (except perhaps a coterie audience) is to wrap important questions of the play in oblique and abstruse symbolism. This is not to imply that imagery and symbolism have no place in the theater, but rather to suggest that their proper function is a subordinate one: to enrich the language and support the action. There is ample room for complexity in dramatic verse as long as it underlies a lucid surface; but the complexity should inform and amplify the matter, not obfuscate it. Perhaps it is for these reasons that T. S. Eliot, though something of an imagist in his more cryptic non-dramatic poems, turned to rhetorical verse in *Murder in the Cathedral,* adopting, by the way, the Classical practice of *imitatio,* for by his own acknowledgment he patterned much of his style in that play on *Everyman* (ca. 1500). The stylistic influence of Greek tragedy, moreover, may be seen in his choruses. In *Murder in the Cathedral* Eliot's style is not simple, but it is both clear and eloquent.

The fairly recent notion that rhetorical verse is less than poetic is flatly contradicted by the evidence of literary history. Most major poems and verse plays numbered among the classics have been composed on a base of rhetoric; they are characteristically eloquent and not opaque and therefore stylistically suitable for dramatic, narrative, and reflective forms. Rhetoric is nothing less than the art of eloquence. C. S. Lewis calls it "the darling of humanity, *soavissima,* as Dante says, 'the sweetest of all the other sciences.'" He then reflects upon a truth that contemporary critics seldom take into account:

> Nearly all our older poetry was written and read
> by men to whom the distinction between poetry
> and rhetoric . . . would have been meaningless.[10]

In recent times writers who have drawn upon the resources of rhetoric have all too often incurred the somewhat vague charge of insincerity. The charge is false. It would be difficult to find a speech more rich in stylistic rhetoric than Abraham Lincoln's "Gettysburg Address." Among the schemes and tropes Lincoln artfully used in that brief masterpiece are hyperbaton, metaphor, anaphora, antithesis, epistrophe, and ploce. If it was the ethos of Linclon himself that rendered the speech sincere, it was his eloquence that gave form and expression to his sincerity and made the speech memorable.

I am convinced that those who underestimate the importance of rhetoric in Western literature (Classical rhetoric I mean, not the new inexpensive kind) know little about it or nothing at all. To put it another way, those who disdain the art, like those who disdain formal grammar, do so out of ignorance and therefore ought to be regarded with charitable forbearance.

Some critics imagine that verse drama is an exhausted genre, but the idea that a genre can be exhausted is too facile to be taken seriously. It is a cliché that raises far more questions than it presumes to answer. Doubtless, valid reasons may be found to account for changing tastes and declining—or increasing—interest in one genre or

---

10. *English Literature in the Sixteenth Century* (Oxford University Press, 1954), p. 61.

another, but exhaustion is rarely among them. In speaking of a particular of Aristotelian criticism, William K. Wimsatt and Cleanth Brooks maintained that

> Jonson furnishes . . . lively demonstration,
> through free and virile Englishing, how little the
> classic mind thought that previous realization of
> an idea could tarnish it.[11]

One might also remark how little the classic mind thought, or *thinks,* that previous realization of a genre or a verse form could tarnish it.

Maugham, himself a distinguished prose playwright of the early century, deplored the decline of verse drama:

> To my mind, the drama took a wrong turning
> when the demand for realism led it to abandon
> the ornament of verse. Verse has a specific
> dramatic value as anyone can see by observing in
> himself the thrilling effect of a tirade in one of
> Racine's plays or of any of Shakespeare's great set
> pieces; . . . it is due to the emotional power of
> rhythmical speech. But more than that: verse
> forces on the matter a conventional form that
> heightens the aesthetic effect. . . But the chief
> value of verse is that it delivers a play from sober
> reality. It puts it on another level, at one remove
> from life, and so makes it easier for the audience
> to attune themselves to that state of feeling in
> which they are most susceptible to the drama's
> specific appeal.[12]

The realistic media of contemporary verse and diction are not ideally suited to a Grecian mythic theme. It is through classic diction and blank verse that I have sought to create a formal distance between the audience and the play and

---

11. *Literary Criticism: A Short History* (University of Chicago Press, 1957), Vol. II, p. 727.
12. Maugham, pp. 140–41.

thereby heighten the action and engage more fully the emotional and intellectual empathy of the audience.

Observing the principle of *decorum*, I have adopted classic diction because it is appropriate to my theme. The classic diction of English poetry is, of course, the Elizabethan idiom, the instrument not only of England's golden age of literature, but of most of the poetry written before the present century: the language of Marlowe and Shakespeare is in most essentials the language of Milton and Pope, of Keats and Tennyson. James Sutherland said somewhere that Elizabethan English "must be the envy of anyone who puts pen to paper." At its best, it is highly vigorous and possesses a syntactical plasticity that is no longer possible in today's English. That no recent translation of the Bible approaches the literary merit of either the Authorized Version (1611) or the Rheims-Douay version (O.T. 1582, N.T. 1609) can be attributed not only to the disparate tastes and talents of the translators, but also to the qualities inherent in their language.

W. H. Auden, in his introduction to *The Oxford Book of Light Verse*, observes that although Wordsworth expressly intended to write in a language such as common men speak, "whenever he tries to do so he is not completely successful, while in his best work, the *Odes* and *The Prelude*, his diction is poetic, and far removed from the spoken word." Classic, or poetic, diction survived into the early years of the present century. Later it was adopted by such poets as Dorothy Sayers in her translation of *The Divine Comedy* (1949–56) and by Lacy Lockert in his blank verse translation of Corneille's chief works (Princeton, 1957).

Current bias against blank verse notwithstanding, I have not thought it worth while to consider using any other verse form in either play, for I cannot conceive of any other that would suit my purposes as well. In the *Princeton Encyclopedia of Poetry and Poetics*, Samuel Levin calls blank verse "the distinctive poetic form of our language . . . the medium of nearly all verse drama and of much narrative and reflective verse." Though it has been neglected by contemporary poets, to dismiss the form as obsolete would be precipitate, to say the least. As Levin reminds us, blank verse has been employed by such major poets of this century as Eliot (in *The Waste Land*), Frost, and Auden. Yeats used it in eleven of the fifteen short verse plays he wrote between 1904 and 1939, as well as in most of his dramatic and narrative poems. If more recent poets seldom write blank verse, they also seldom write long poems, of which blank verse has been the dominant medium. When they do attempt them, they typically adopt less disciplined forms; but recent attempts to supplant blank verse with new prosodic experiments have proved less than successful. They have usually resulted in hybrid forms that waver uncertainly between prosaic verse and poetic prose. When adopting these new forms, poets tend to avoid poetic flights and steer a safer course; but in attempting little, they achieve less. If Arnold in 1860 could successfully use blank verse and classic diction and emulate Homer besides without incurring the opprobrium of critics then or now, it should very well remain possible in our time to utilize the great literary conventions without offending the sensibilities of serious readers, except perhaps those of the more dogmatic of modernists, whose censure is often praise.

Blank verse, whenever it has happened to be written well, retains its freshness, its flexibility, and its power to please us and move us, and no quantity of bad blank verse has diminished the pre-eminent beauty and usefulness of the form itself. I therefore felt no compulsion to cast about in search of some experimental, exotic, or doctrinal verse form in order to accomplish what could be better accomplished by a form already at hand, fully developed and proved, and singularly effective.

I believe that the reasons usually proposed to discard literary and other artistic forms are specious. It is no more likely to exhaust an important verse form than it is to exhaust a literary genre. In academic circles it has become

axiomatic that a revolution in science or politics will precipitate a revolution in the arts, after which poetry can
neither be written nor read in the same way. The premise
is doubtful. One cannot easily imagine what invention, dis-
covery, or movement of the last ten or twelve decades could
swiftly lay to rest the accumulated cultural experience of
twenty-five centuries of Western civilization. It is most unlikely that Einsteinian physics or Freudian psychology or
Marxist socialism has appreciably altered the course of
literary history. To consider the evidence of the last century, one need only inquire what effect the industrial revolution or the scientific revolution had on Tennyson's "In
Memoriam" or on Arnold's "Thyrsis." Either of these
poems could just as well have been composed before the
construction of the railroads or the publication of *On the
Origin of the Species*. The universal themes of our literature
are concerned with human nature—the thoughts and
passions, the virtues and vices of mankind: *quod ubique,
quod semper, quod ab omnibus creditum est,* "what is always,
what is everywhere, and what is by all men believed." The
events and innovations of the present century have not
altered the way we read—or ought to read—literature of
the past, nor is there any compelling reason why they must
alter the way we read or write literature of the present, in
spite of what recent critics may say.

V

When is a critic not a critic? In his presidential address of
1932 delivered before the Bibliographic Society, Sir William W. Gregg said that there is a point where textual
criticism "changes its nature and becomes metacritical."[13]
Jacques Barzun suggests that when a critic becomes so
esoteric that he no longer communicates with the general

---

13. "Bibliography—A Retrospect," *The Bibliographic Society, 1892–
1942: Studies in Retrospect* (London: Bibliographic Society, 1945),
p. 30.

reader, he is not a critic at all, but belongs "to some other guild." The critics Barzun charges are "the high theorists of our day—structuralists, semioticists, deconstructionists, and others." He adds:

> Each practitioner has his own vocabulary of his own making and believes it alone capable of producing profound discoveries. The late Roland Barthes expressly disparaged clarity, saying that after Marx and Freud complexity had ruled out the clear and simple. The argument is naive. One could also say that after Pythagoras or after the medieval scholastics, the human mind was doomed to eternal complexity and perplexity. The argument is also specious, because it assumes that all art is a riddle to unravel. . . . [14]

The general reader once approached a critic in hopes of finding an interpreter, one who would illuminate a text and act as a catalyst between the author and the reader; but today's critics have abandoned such useful functions in favor of more metaphysical pursuits. The "high theorists" have acquired a virtuosity that may impress and stimulate a certain kind of scholar, but it is a virtuosity that is of small consequence to the general reader. The criticism produced by these theorists has little to do with literature as Dante and Shakespeare knew it. Like Barzun, Ellul regards their labors with a doubtful eye:

> Virtuosity has never been a substitute for truth. Withdrawal into virtuosity of this kind only shows that [for them] there is no longer any such thing as truth. [15]

The author of *Das Kapital* was not one to esteem tradition, whether political or literary. However worthy his literary criticism may be judged, it is well to keep in mind

---

14. "A Little Matter of Sense," *New York Times Book Review,* 21 June 1987, p. 28.
15. Ellul, p. 197.

that objective inquiry is hardly the métier of a revolutionary ideologue. Karl Marx thought that what men are and
how they express themselves depend on how they live. He
regarded men as products of their own experience in a
contemporary world, but failed to see that what literate
men are, how they read, and how they express themselves
depend more on what they have been and on what they
have read—their past, their historical and cultural antecedents. Even in a democratic state it is the most literate
segment of society, not the masses and not necessarily the
wealthy, that produces and cultivates the arts of civilization
and transmits them to posterity; and literate men, above
others, are products of a long and complex past far more
than they are products of the present and their own circumscribed experience in a contemporary world.

In an age of stability and confidence, culture is dis-
seminated among a public predisposed to emulate the
taste and manners of the more enlightened members of
society. In such a time artists and intellectuals are more
likely to rise from the masses and bolster the forces of
civilized culture. Such was the condition in Periclean
Athens, Augustan Rome, and Renaissance Florence, and
such was the condition in Elizabethan London as Hamlet
had occasion to note in what is obviously a contemporary
reference: "The age is grown so picked that the toe of the
peasant comes so near the heel of the courtier, he galls
his kibe." High culture is less likely to survive and prosper
when it departs from universality and becomes the private
preserve of a coterie detached and removed from the
public.

VI

Literature as art is made possible by what Samuel Johnson
called "community of mind," a common pool of knowledge that is of vital importance in the discourse of civilized men and women, a cultural heritage shared by a
literate public that constitutes a significant portion of the

population. In the West that heritage is both Classical and Judeo-Christian, though not in equal measure. An author has scope to work within the literary tradition only when he can assume his readers share a familiarity with that tradition and its conventions and with the broader cultural heritage upon which they rest. As the familiarity is diminished, however, communication becomes constricted and literature as high art enters a period of decline. Literary allusion and historical reference, which enriched the literature of our language in past centuries, has been all but abandoned in our time. Forty-five years ago, James Sutherland ascribed the change to an unlettered public and, ultimately, to "a shift in emphasis in education." Before the present age few literary allusions required glosses in the text, for a community of mind obtained; it informed the eloquence of earlier times, eloquence in the speeches of the great and in the letters of the humble. Following are two typical examples of allusion—one historical, the other literary—of a kind that would now be unlikely.

On the eve of the Civil War, Senator Robert Toombs of Georgia addressed the Senate (January 7, 1861). South Carolina had become the first state to secede, and Toombs cautioned against a Federal resort to arms, saying:

> The greater majority of . . . sister states . . .
> consider her cause as their cause; and I charge
> you in their name today, "Touch not Saguntum."

"Touch not Saguntum." It was unnecessary for Toombs to explain that the Carthaginian siege of Saguntum, a Spanish city under the protection of Rome, was the immediate cause of the Second Punic War, a war that proved fatal to Carthage. The implication was not lost on the United States Senate of 1861.

Though a community of mind persists in our time, it does so in a precarious way. The following example containing a literary allusion is an instance drawn from more recent years. In 1939 a German submarine penetrated the defenses of Scapa Flow, the base of the Home Fleet, and sank the battleship *Royal Oak*. (Sir) Winston Churchill, referring to the loss in a speech he delivered as First Lord of the Admiralty, saluted the enemy U-boat commander with these magnanimous words: "Even the ranks of Tuscany / Could scarce forbear to cheer." Churchill rightly assumed that Britons hearing his speech would recognize these familiar lines from "Horatius at the Bridge" from Lord Macaulay's *Lays of Ancient Rome,* a work that had been common fare in the schools for many years—not a great work, perhaps, but an eloquent expression of a noble legend, a shared heritage, and therefore part of the community of mind.

Community of mind as a centripetal force in our society and culture began to erode even as early as the last half of the eighteenth century. Wordsworth, in his preface to the *Lyrical Ballads* (1798), recognized the extent of that change:

> A multitude of causes, unknown to former times,
> are now acting with a combined force to blunt the
> discriminating powers of the mind, and, unfitting
> it for all voluntary exertion, to reduce it to a state
> of almost savage torpor.

The effect of this change, said Wordsworth, is a popular craving for inferior literature of a sensational character, "which rapid communication of intelligence hourly gratifies . . . and the invaluable works of our elder writers are driven into neglect." Although the causes are undoubtedly complex, the erosion of community of mind progressed with the advent of the industrial revolution and the rise of *mass culture,*[16] and it was accelerated in the early twentieth century by that intellectual and moral relativism which laid the groundwork for the anarchic 1960's and 70's, when the integrity of Western civilization was severely shaken by a new barbarism. What relativism and skepticism undermine, nihilism destroys. "We are living," said

---

16. A notorious oxymoron of recent coinage.

Lionel Abel, "in an age of nihilism, cultural nihilism"[17] (cf. Ellul's "blind negation," above). It is a road to nowhere.

As our cultural ties with the past grow increasingly tenuous, the community of mind which long nurtured and sustained literature and the other arts of the Occident continues to decline towards something resembling that long gothic night which descended upon the civilized world fifteen hundred years ago. Art divorced and severed from the past—from tradition, convention, and all that a cultural heritage implies—is art that is destined to be born and buried on the same day. Perhaps no parochialism is more confining or more stifling than that of the present: the parochialism of the modernist who would annul the past, spurn the masters, and think all art begins with him. "Forget the past," said Sir Winston Churchill, "and you lose the future." It is an observation that applies as much to art as it does to politics or, indeed, to civilization itself.

The continued fragmentation of education (or what passes for education) has inevitably contributed to the further abatement of community of mind and that sense of continuity without which civilization cannot survive. Soon after Charles W. Eliot became President of Harvard University in 1869, he began to revolutionize higher education. Following the German model, rather than the English, and emphasizing practical sciences at the expense of humanities, he changed the university into a school for specialists. One by one the colleges of America followed Harvard's example; consequently, as Van Wyck Brooks and Otto Bettmann reflected, in their embrace of science and technology colleges neglected the classics "to the detriment of first-rate writing" and, even more significantly, to the detriment of educating "spacious men."[18] Educators came to regard literature as something of an academic ornament—as if literacy had little to do with civilization.

---

17. *Important Nonsense* (Buffalo, N. Y.: Prometheus Books, 1987), p. 147.
18. *Our Literary Heritage* (New York: Dutton, 1956), pp. 156–57.

More recently, university English departments, yielding to special interest groups, are allowing themselves to be changed into yet another branch of the social sciences. A new form of fragmentation called *multiculturalism,* or *pluralism,* is displacing from the curriculum much of an already depleted store of the classics and promises to diminish further what little is left of community of mind. Like Chaos in the *Dunciad,*

> Thus at her felt approach, and secret might,
> *Art* after *art* goes out, and all is Night.

In our classrooms the great books are being replaced by politically correct literature, mostly of a contemporary, provincial, and ephemeral kind—all in the name of cultural equality. Egalitarianism, *reductus ad absurdum,* may yet finish the ruin of that which technological education began. As intellectual centers of high culture, our universities have become much discredited.

Less than fifty years ago, most college graduates could still be recognized by their ability to speak and write articulately. Standards have since fallen so far that it may be said we are living in a non-literate society. Although bookstores are stocked with more titles than ever before, comparatively few have anything to do with serious literature; most convey information of a practical or technical nature. But all information is not of equal price, nor is all information equally conducive to liberal education or to the good life, as Aristotle defined it. It is not the conveyance of practical information that produces what Brooks and Bettmann called the "spacious man." A more technologically advanced society is not necessarily a more civilized society. "It is better," said Epictetus, "that great men live in small houses than that small men live in great houses." Mr. Dooley, the sage bartender of Archie Road, expressed a similar thought eighty years ago when, unimpressed by the wonders of modern technology that were beginning to create the New York skyline, he said, "I want to see sky-scrapin' men. But I won't."[19]

Poetry cannot easily survive in an age of technology and materialism when schools and universities have so neglected the humanities that the resulting decline in literacy has reduced the audience for poetry. In the face of that reduction, most contemporary poets continue to indulge their eccentricities and write for a coterie rather than a public audience. Apart from captive student-readers, there remains a significant if small audience for the poetic literature of the past, and that audience may be drawn upon by contemporary poets who can communicate to them. The foremost poets of this century—Yeats, Auden, Frost, and Wilbur among them—have also been, like major poets of the past, articulate and accessible; but poets of modernist schools have been no more successful in finding a public audience today than their avant-garde predecessors were two or three generations past. The cynosure and battle-cry of the Renaissance humanists was *ad fontes,* "to the sources." If poets would once again turn to the Classical fountainheads of the art and recover some measure of the eloquence and sanity of the ancients, which poetry began losing even before the advent of this troubled century, then might poetry reclaim among the literate its former station in the van of literature.

---

19. Finley Peter Dunne, "Machinery," *Mr. Dooley on Ivrything and Ivrybody* (New York: Dover, 1963), p. 200.

A NOTE ON THE TEXT

In verbs ending in *ed,* I have followed the usual custom of indicating unsounded *ed* by *'d;* however, I have at the same time reverted to the practice now fallen into disuse of indicating sounded *ed* by the grave accent *(èd)*. Although poets and editors generally adopt only one of these devices, I have preferred to combine them in order to assist the actor or reader as much as possible in "hearing" what he reads, for the verse should either be spoken aloud or heard in the mind's ear.

Since there is obviously no need to employ the accent in *ed* terminations usually sounded in modern speech (e.g., *beloved*), I have not supplied it. I have also retained unsounded *ed,* rather than render it *'d,* when *e* affects the pronunciation of the preceding consonant (e.g., *raged,* rather than *rag'd*) or the preceding vowel (e.g., *hoped,* rather than *hop'd*).

I have indicated possessive nouns terminating in the sibilants *ce* and *x,* as well as both monosyllabic and polysyllabic possessive nouns terminating in *s,* by an apostrophe without a successive *s* (e.g., *justice' sake, Styx' black brim,* and *Zeus' decree,* rather than *justice's sake, Styx's black brim,* and *Zeus's decree*). I have, of course, adopted this familiar enough convention for the sake of euphony: to avoid the unpleasing apposition of sibilants.

In some few instances I have employed anapestic substitution in the initial foot of a line following one with masculine ending; if the first two syllables of the foot (always beginning with a monosyllabic preposition or coordinating conjunction) were to be erroneously scanned as a trochee, the line would appear to be a hexameter. I have, however, more frequently resorted to trochaic and spondaic substitution, especially in the initial foot. For dramatic or lyrical purposes I have occasionally employed the short line—usually iambic trimeter.

In stressing the proper syllable or syllables in words that may be accented in more ways than one (e.g., *contumely, secreted, into, unto*), the reader should be guided by the metrical context: the cadences of the lines in which such words as these appear. This same principle applies to the number of syllables a word may contain; for instance, *Orpheus* (like *Juliet* or *Romeo* in Shakespeare's play) is sometimes disyllabic and sometimes trisyllabic.

The Golden Lyre

A Tragedy in Three Acts

PERSONS OF THE DRAMA

- NARRATOR
- ORPHEUS
- CHORUS OF SHEPHERDS
- EURYDICE
- FIRST SHEPHERD
- SECOND SHEPHERD
- CHARON
- SPIRIT
- CHORUS OF SPIRITS
- HADES
- PERSEPHONE

Invocation

All ye Pierian Muses that haunt the slopes
Of snowy Pindus to Dium's sounding shore,
Unloose the flood-gates of my brooding heart:
Undam the tears that swell mine eyes with sorrow
As I recall to mind the hapless lot
Of fair Eurydice and the depthless grief
Of Oeagrus' son, whose golden lyre once charm'd
The rushing streams to cease their seaward flow
And the winds to pause so men might hear
His noble song; whose music well-timber'd *Argo*
Moved upon Poseidon's wide domain—
Far sailing *Argo*, first sea-taming ship.
Sing, ye Muses, sing of him whose tongue
Against the daemon wards of Dis prevail'd;
And send forth, spouting, Castalian founts to flood
The sapless veins of my expositor.
Deign to kindle with some quickening spirit
These dark and tragic scenes that I would limn
With an untutor'd pen. My feeble murmurs
Strive amain to rise from earth, but fall
Ere they begin their flight. Yet by your breath,
Blest maids, do metamorphose these frail numbers—
Not into stately and exsurgent sounds
That mount up high like blasts from Triton's horn
To charge the air and smite the azure dome,
But to those gentler strains that shepherds sing
To beguile the darker hours and calm their flocks
Upon the lower slopes of steep Parnassus.

ACT I

Scene i

[*House lights out, curtain remains closed, apron dimly lighted. Narrator enters from right, crosses down right centre to apron and stands in gradually brightened light as he begins addressing audience in clear, well modulated speech, neither too conversational nor too declamatory.*]

NARRATOR

In fair Pieria our tragedy begins,
In times not ancient, as these our latter days
(For never was the world as old as now),
But in that time when Zeus enthronèd sat
Among the lesser gods on blue Olympus—
When the world was young, the forests wide,
The seas unsullied, and brighter shone the stars.
Let three and thirty centuries retrace
Their backward course to that far-off summertime.

[*Pause as curtain rises and* NARRATOR *crosses down right, behind curtain-line. Scene, a vale in Pieria.* EURYDICE *asleep in a bower and not visible to audience.* NARRATOR *continues speaking.*]

Here in this pleasant vale a maiden lies.
She sleeps and dreams on this her bridal day,
And to her bower the happy bridegroom comes.
Little does he think what grim mischance

The day unfolds. On her is all his mind,
On her that holds his joyful heart in thrall.

[*Enter* ORPHEUS *and* CHORUS OF SHEPHERDS; *then exit*
NARRATOR.]

ORPHEUS

What, Eurydice, not stirring yet?
How lovely in sleep she lies!
Behold how Dawn, rising from her couch
Of gold, doth stretch her shining arms to greet
The day and brighten all this fruitful land
Thrice blest for thy fair presence.
Ope thy veilèd eyes and banish Sleep,
Death's younger sister, she that steals the hours
And keeps from us a thousand sweet delights.

CHORUS

Arise, chaste nymph, for the evening star that rules
The vaulty night doth fly before the hoofs
Of Phoebus' steeds. Now sleeps the nightingale,
The lark is on the wing, and rich-garb'd Summer
Strows her spices on the gentle wind.

ORPHEUS

Come, Eurydice, thy bridegroom calls thee.
Now breaks the long'd-for hour when we shall wed.
From sleep's thick languor rouse thyself, my love,
And drink the promise of this summer's morn.

[*Exit* CHORUS; *enter from the bower* EURYDICE, *clad in a
white gown.*]

EURYDICE

The charms of sleep dissolve before the music
Of thy voice. Good morrow, my gracious lord.

ORPHEUS

My bride, in white array'd, outshines the dawn.
Fresher than the morning air thou art
And more bewitching than any nymph of Tempe;
And I, the happiest of men, embrace thee.

[*They embrace. As* ORPHEUS *speaks, he leads* EURYDICE *to right centre.*]

Now let us look to greet the wedding guests.
Give me thy hand, Eurydice, and I
Shall lead thee barefoot through the fields still moist
With pale Aurora's tears, and there together
Shall we hail the light of this new day.
The guests are come; the rites await our pleasure.

EURYDICE

Then haste we to the rites. With all my heart
I would that we were wed. And I may say
No maid e'er woke to see a fairer day.

[*Black-out*]

Scene ii

[*Scene, the same; a short time later. Enter from left* FIRST SHEPHERD *and* CHORUS.]

FIRST SHEPHERD

Who is't approaches, as lovely as the moon,
More splendid far than any mortal maid?
The brightness of her garments so becomes her
That one would think some goddess he had seen.
It hath been said celestial Artemis
Will walk the earth on mornings such as this:

Like moonlight gliding o'er a brook she moves.
But lo, it is e'en she that Orpheus loves,
The fair Eurydice, and with her walks
Proud Orpheus. I'll speak with them. Well met!
[*To* ORPHEUS]
Whither goest thou thus merrily?

ORPHEUS

Why, to my wedding, friend. Thou knowest well.

FIRST SHEPHERD

Alas, I had clean forgot. How now, my lady?
Art ready to bestow thy nuptial yoke
About the neck of this unwitting youth?

ORPHEUS

What tyrant would not bow to such a yoke?

EURYDICE

I pray the love I bear for Orpheus
Prove never a yoke for him, but sweet content
And solace all his years.

FIRST SHEPHERD
            Nay, my lady,
I do but jest. This noble match all Hellas
Cheers. But we have tarried here too long.
Let us now rejoice. Begin the rites!

[*Exit* ORPHEUS *with* EURYDICE *and* FIRST SHEPHERD.
CHORUS *remains.*]

CHORUS
    Haste forth, ye bright Pierian maids,
    Through grassy glens and silver glades;
    With wreathèd garlands bind your locks
    And bid the shepherds leave their flocks.

Together wend your merry ways
Through woody slopes where harts do graze;
Nor cease to gather fresh-blown flowers
From shady meads 'neath leafy bowers.
Do garner daisies, tender-stemm'd,
And royal violets, close-hemm'd,
And rosebuds ruddy as the dawn.
Near the brook where drinks the fawn
Pluck sweet narcissi, nor do ye fail
To sweep up gorgeous lilies, pale
As frosty dew. Prepare the feast!
And make ye merry, man and beast.
Sing io to Hymen. Io, io Hymen.

LEADER OF THE CHORUS

Prepare the hymeneal feast: bring berries,
Cakes and nuts and ruby cherries,
Roasted viands and russet wine
And azure grapes torn from the vine.
Top the board with linens rare,
And thereon spread the fragrant fare.

CHORUS

Deck the board with fresh-pluck'd laurel,
Interspers'd with festoons floral.
Make ye merry, all ye shepherds,
Maids and swains and well-girt goatherds,
For Orpheus most blissfully
This day doth wed Eurydice.
Sing io to Hymen. Io, io Hymen!

[*Exit* CHORUS; *black out.*]

Scene iii

[Scene, the same. Enter NARRATOR.*]*

NARRATOR

By Orpheus' heaven-favour'd voice invok'd,
Hymenaeus in his saffron mantle sped
Through aery space to bless the nuptial rites.
But tardily Hymenaeus arriv'd—
Tardily and inauspiciously;
For his brand did smoke and darkly sputter,
And therefore were his looks sore troubled.
                                    Yet Orpheus
Heeded not the omen. The rites were done,
And now the beauteous maid was his to cherish,
Was his to love; in deathless love conjoin'd
They were. On these delightful thoughts he dwelt
And on no other, for soaring was his spirit,
And nothing more but these delightful thoughts
Would his mind contain. Soon stray'd they from
                                    the guests,
This blissful, happy pair, and from each other:
Eurydice, laughing mongst her sister nymphs,
Went off into a wood; Orpheus,
Attended by a hoary-headed shepherd
With whom it was his wont oft-times to speak,
Confiding in the wise though rustic man,
Wander'd into a meadow.

[Enter ORPHEUS *and* FIRST SHEPHERD.*]*

                          As they were holding
Converse there together, the old man rais'd
His eyes and pointed toward the wood, saying:

FIRST SHEPHERD

Look, where out of the forest's bordering brakes
A frantic shepherd hastens.

ORPHEUS

          He comes this way
And runs as he were chased by fifty furies.

[*Enter* SECOND SHEPHERD.]

SECOND SHEPHERD

Oh, Orpheus, my lord!

ORPHEUS

          What is it, man?
Thou makest signs to speak, but sayest nothing.

FIRST SHEPHERD

He's dumb for want of breath.

ORPHEUS

               Then rest thee here
Until thy breath return to thee. But what
Dread tidings do I read in thy twisted visage?
What news lies hid beneath thy wrinkled brow?

SECOND SHEPHERD

My lord, Eurydice, your beauteous bride,
Lies dying, by a venomous serpent stung!
She calls for you.

NARRATOR

          His words were darts of ice
That rudely did transfix the poet's breast,
Freezing to numbness all his senses. And he
Was stricken dumb and stared with sightless eyes.

[*Exit* ORPHEUS, *followed by the rest. Curtain drop.*]

Scene iv

[*Scene, a grove sacred to Artemis. Near a small stone altar,* EURYDICE *lies dying. Enter* CHORUS *and* NARRATOR.]

CHORUS

Most mighty son of Cronus, Olympus' king,
Who with thy crashing thunder cleavest the air,
Who with thy sulphurous fires smitest the pines,
Dashing to earth their loftiest limbs, receive
Our plea: Take pity on a guiltless pair
That ne'er gainsaid a word of thy grave ord'nance,
Nor did thee ill in deed or secret thought.
Let Death look to the impious, who flout
Thy laws and scorn thy wrath, and let him look
To the weary agèd, sated with life's feast;
But let him spare this maid that honours thee
And does thee reverence. An mercy sit
Within thy breast, wilt thou yet suffer Death
To cast his sable mantle o'er the eyes
Of young Eurydice? O royal father
Of the gods, we pray thee, lift up thy hand
In ruth and stay the ruthless hand of Death.

[*As Narrator speaks, enter* ORPHEUS. *He stands, then kneels, before* EURYDICE.]

NARRATOR

To a wooded vale where stands an altar sacred
To the virgin huntress, Orpheus runs
Like a wounded stag made mad with terror's spur;
And in that vale he sees Eurydice
Lying motionless upon the earth
Midst flowers that she glean'd for Diane's shrine—
More lovely than those scatter'd blooms is she.
Seeing her thus, the grieving bard cries out:

ORPHEUS

Oh how the sight of this assails mine eyes!
Jealous gods, what mischief have ye wrought!

NARRATOR

Now kneels he by her side to kiss her cheek,
Whereat she stirs and feebly opes her eyes.

(*Crosses up stage right to unlighted area.*)

EURYDICE

Orpheus, is it thou?

ORPHEUS

Ay, sweet maid.
How fares my bride?

EURYDICE

So thou be'st near me, well.

ORPHEUS

The blood that quits thy cheeks belies thy words.
Uneasy sits my heart.
Ah, what sweet dew is that which clouds thine eyes?

EURYDICE

By these welling tears do I entreat
Fortuna to forswear her dread decree
That would perforce unbind me from thine arms.
The goddess has o'erleap'd all earthly bounds
In gracing me with more than mortal crown.
Ay, that my joy o'ertopp'd the tallest cedar
And my hopes did dwarf cloud-sundering peaks
Did she soon know, and now she plucks me down.

ORPHEUS

But thou, compounded not of mortal clay,
Art heaven's child. A goddess cannot die.

EURYDICE

I came from out Tithea's muddy womb,
Whereto must I return. Most noble youth,
All my divinity is in thy love.
Alas, I cannot draw my breath to speak.

ORPHEUS

Eurydice!

EURYDICE

Death, oh, thy touch is cold.

[*dies*]

ORPHEUS

What heavy-heavèd groan is that? And dost
Thou suck the sweetness of the air no more?
Those lustrous eyes grow dim, and they do stare
As if seeing naught but dark and empty air.

[*Enter* FIRST SHEPHERD.]

FIRST SHEPHERD

Raving fiends of hell, abate your rage,
For now you've wrought your utmost felony!

ORPHEUS

Traitorous eyes, your black report is false.
Will you still look upon this grievous sight
And not be struck with all-obscuring night?

CHORUS

Thou who wast wont to sing thy joyous paeons
Must needs retune thy lyre to darker strains;
For she, the maid that thou hast ta'en to wife,
Is even now betrothed to Death. Alas,
Her nuptial garments are her funeral robes.

ORPHEUS

She was more dear to me than life itself,
And that I knew while she was mine; and yet
I knew not ere this day how much I loved.

FIRST SHEPHERD

Never have I seen a maid so fair.
But only an hour ago I did observe
How warm the rose of youth blush'd in her cheeks,
And now——

ORPHEUS

See how that rose lies crush'd and paled.

CHORUS

Never will she waken to behold
Hyperion's bright and wreathèd brow as he,
Fair god, exhorts flame-pinion'd coursers charging
Fast across the saffron field of dawn.
Where were ye, dryads, when Eurydice
Did kneel in worship at your mistress' shrine?
Where were ye when the craven serpent stung her?

LEADER OF THE CHORUS

O virgin goddess,
Dost thou seek thy child? thy fairest dove?
Ah, gentle huntress, seek no more, for lo—
Here lies she dead. Now lay aside thy quiver
And unstring thy bow, and weep; yea, weep
Till all the forest echoes with thy wail.

CHORUS

Arise, ye dozing naiads, rise and weep.
Eurydice is dead. With tears augment
Your sylvan springs and pools until the waters
Top their banks and drench the shaded vale.

ORPHEUS

Earth-shaking volcanoes, spew forth lava! Encompass
All the world with a thick and ashen shroud!
And thou, bright sun, look on this hollow round
No more, nor fringe with fire snow-robèd crests,
Nor raise thy head above the watery plain
Where stout-ribb'd barks breast the swelling flood.
Let darkness cover all!

FIRST SHEPHERD

What, must we all perish for thy loss?
Alas, my lord, thou railest at the winds.
It is thy grief that speaks and not thy reason.

ORPHEUS

Wast thou not the serpent, Death? Then meet
It is that thou a worm shouldst counterfeit,
A lowly worm that grovels in the dust
And filth, that strikes all suddenly, unseen,
With not a breath of warning. Sages and kings
Alike thou slayest, goodly men and just,
And yet thou'lt suffer to live the noisome vermin
That feast upon their poor remains. And now,
Thou merciless sunderer, most foully hast
Thou slain a lovely maiden, green in years.

FIRST SHEPHERD

Her life was brief, my lord, and so her sorrows.
Thine have just begun.
He that laid his icy hand upon her
Keeps no calendar, but comes to all,
Late and betimes, the agèd and the young.

ORPHEUS

Thou who mak'st thy presence sharply felt,
But timorously conceal'st thy countenance,

Assume some shape that I might thee perceive.
Insatiable and overweening fiend,
Affect whatever protean forms thou wilt
And, being palpable, confront me here!
Then shalt thou vanquish'd be and Death shall die.

FIRST SHEPHERD

Unhappy youth, allay thy errant rage.
Give sorrow scope enough and mourn awhile,
For it is meet and just to mourn thy loss,
But quell these venom'd humours that nothing breed
Save further detriment.

ORPHEUS

Mourn awhile?
Ay, that. While I have tears and breath I'll mourn.
There lies my love, Beauty's paragon,
Whose ivory visage, heaven-tutoring,
Still dims the blaze of golden Helios.
See how her locks in fair profusion flow
In liquid streams. Shimmering in the sun
Like molten gold, they pour upon her breasts.
How gently sighs the wind through her soft locks,
As if she lie asleep, so might I swear—
But no, 'tis all a ruse of empty air.
Peace, ye caressing winds that from this form
Do swiftly rob the last remaining warmth;
Stir not thus my fair love's silken tresses,
For thus stir ye false hope within my breast.
How dancing locks do mock that silent head!—
As if they knew not yet her life is shed.
Now fly, false hope, for she will never wake.
These eyes, through which Love shot his shafts of fire
That found their mark in my unworthy breast,
Are forever closed, and I shall never see
Their light again.

FIRST SHEPHERD
You will trace their beauty
In the stars.

ORPHEUS
The stars are far remote
And cold to me.

FIRST SHEPHERD
Still lovely in death she is.

ORPHEUS
Immortal Beauty's only mortal child
By a fathomless flood of night is swallow'd.
How well it pleased my heart to see her smile.
Lo, how quick the colour flies those lips
Wherethrough she spoke to me in accents soft.
In vain they're parted. Death has robb'd her breath.

[A pause. NARRATOR moves to right centre, then speaks.]

NARRATOR
Thus Orpheus mourn'd. So sorely griev'd he was,
The music that had stay'd the running brook,
Unfix'd the oaks, and charm'd the feral beasts
Could not console or comfort him that made it.

CHORUS
The boist'rous winds of winter yield to spring,
Which soon the fervent summer puts to rout.
Fruitful autumn then succeeds the summer,
Laying her to rest with fallen leaves.
Again chill winter freezes all to stillness.
And what the seasons taint or take away
The changing moon restores, and Nature wakes
To walk abroad. The trees send forth their leaves,
The grass doth rise, and flowers bloom anew.

All things revive in nature but wretched man:
Once gone, he is no more than dust and ashes.
His voice is heard no more.
The glorious sun in his diurnal course
And all the other stars that crown the night
Shall never see his vanish'd face again.

[*Exit* CHORUS *with* NARRATOR. *After a brief pause,* FIRST
SHEPHERD *speaks.*]

FIRST SHEPHERD

Wilt thou come along, my lord? How dost thou?

ORPHEUS

I never knew till now what sorrow is.
When she grew cold, Death—striking with his dart—
Tore the warmth from my still-beating heart.
And yet I live, but have no will to live.
Then welcome night.
Ah, ruthless Fortune, rudely hast thou thrust me
From thy wheel. Upon the barren earth
Deject I lie; no lower can I fall.
Nor thee nor aught fear I, nor even death,
For happy is the death which endeth sorrow.
He fears no rack that lieth in his grave.

FIRST SHEPHERD

What, thinkest thou this senseless clay
Can hear thy plaints or feel one burning tear?

ORPHEUS

Mark those eyes. Lies there no mind within?

FIRST SHEPHERD

No. Upon those cold and sightless eyes
A thousand sorrows cannot rouse one tear.

ORPHEUS

Peace! Say not this form is but base clay,
Senseless earth and dumb. Urge it not,
I charge thee, for I swear 'tis yet divine,
And yet I know this silent maid's a corpse.
Sometimes I think my mind deceiveth me
And that which merely seems to be is not.
Belike it only seems this maid's a corpse
Or that I dream or have a touch of madness,
And when I wake I'll see my love again.
My head doth reel. Uncertain are my senses.

FIRST SHEPHERD

It availeth thee naught to stop thine ears to reason.
I do but speak some truths to blunt thy passion,
Showing thee a glass wherein thou mayest
View this virulent grief for his true cast.
My words I mean for remedy, not hurt:
Effectual physic though they burn like salt
Pour'd on a fester'd wound.

ORPHEUS

How mend a broken heart? Is't possible?
I understand thy kind intent, old man,
And thank thee for thy counsel, but words of comfort,
Be they proffer'd ne'er so feelingly,
Could never soft the shock of this fell day
Nor any portion of my grief assuage.

FIRST SHEPHERD

Then let these fiery humours rage: consort
With sorrow; wear her faded livery.
These humours will in time themselves consume.
If nothing else, then time will surely mend.

ORPHEUS

How doth time mend a sorrow but in sending
Newer griefs to writhe in hot contention

With the old till they predominate?
And thus, grief-laden, must we wend our way
Until at last we reach the grave's dark brim
Whereat, 'tis thought, all mortal sorrows end.

FIRST SHEPHERD

Thy way is not so baleful as thou thinkest;
Only fresh misfortune colours it so.
One time brings hurt, another time doth mend.
The mightiest griefs are vanquishèd by Time,
Who will anon relieve thy anguish'd breast.

ORPHEUS

Time doth creep when weigh'd with Sorrow's burden.

FIRST SHEPHERD

Alas, thou art but young——

ORPHEUS

                           But old in sorrow.

FIRST SHEPHERD

Nay, young in sorrow.

ORPHEUS

                           Sorrow makes me old.

FIRST SHEPHERD

Will make thee old if thou wilt still repine.
Thou hast thy life, and life holds many joys.

ORPHEUS

I pray thee, speak to me no more of joy.
Lurking Sorrow waits in shadows, watchful,
Until she sees us steep'd in happiness:
Then doth she leap on us with all her might,

Foreknowing well her sting is sharpest then.
And thus is Joy the servitor of Sorrow.

FIRST SHEPHERD

Resign thyself, for in this case there is
No cure. Play not the fool. Eurydice
Is dead, my lord. She's dead, and there's an end.
There is no more to say.

ORPHEUS

Eurydice is dead. Oh, how those words
Of horror rudely hammer at mine ears!
How those words do echo through the caverns
Of my tortured mind!

FIRST SHEPHERD

Unbridled grief
Doth foster raging madness. Will nothing move thee
From this thick and melancholy pall?

ORPHEUS

Only he therefrom can move me—he
That stole her hence.

FIRST SHEPHERD

Soon enough wilt thou die,
Unhappy man, but in the meantime live.

ORPHEUS

Come, thou cloud of black oblivion;
Come enshroud me in eternal night.
Come, sweet sleep of death, and with one sigh
Obliterate a thousand cares.

FIRST SHEPHERD

Alas,
So dark is thy despair? Is't come to this?

ORPHEUS

Tenebrous is the tenor of my woe.

FIRST SHEPHERD

Reverberating through night's cloister'd vaults,
Thy groans do dissipate themselves in air,
Dark lamentations in dark space dissolv'd,
And none save doleful Philomel doth hear.

ORPHEUS

Yet she with her sad wail augments my own.
Thus grief soothes grief, and I am not alone.

FIRST SHEPHERD

Hence with heart-consuming grief! 'Tis strange
How opposites our senses may confound,
For coldest iron seemeth hot when touch'd,
And sharpest pain may smack of pleasure; and so
Methinks thou findest pleasure in thy pain.
I too know grief, and I have trod this earth,
My lord, for thrice as many days as thou.
Pardon me that I must speak it plain,
But 'tis unmanly thus t'indulge thy passion.
Now must thou fix a limit to thy plaints.
Have done, my lord, and stanch thy useless tears.
Thy tears can never call her back from death.

ORPHEUS

My store of tears is spent and I shall weep
No more. 'Tis meet thou chidest me thus. Alas,
Tears will ne'er deliver her from death,
And yet what may my lyre do?
If my music have power to seize men's souls
And even move the trees and senseless stones,
Why then should I not win Eurydice
From Hades' gripe? Ay, to Erebus
Shall I resort, armèd with my lyre.

FIRST SHEPHERD

What wild words are these? Thou needs must die
Ere thou wilt ever see th'infernal shores.

ORPHEUS

No, by Zeus, alive I'll steal my way,
For there is other access to those shores.
'Tis even said that thick and pungent vapours
Issuing from the bowels of certain caves
And fissures in the earth do testify
To such a passage as I might effect.
And hast thou never heard of Heracles,
How he o'ercame the monstrous cur that guards
The Stygian gate and dragg'd him up to earth?

FIRST SHEPHERD

No lusty Heracles art thou, my lord.
Perchance, if thou shouldest reach that land alive,
Thy music lose his wonted charm? What then?
From such a journey thou may'st never return.

ORPHEUS

If there my music lose his charm, why then,
'Tis lost. Howbeit, that I'll essay the quest
I am resolv'd; yea, th' infernal gods
Could not dissuade me from my course. Truly,
Methinks that now I hear her voice again.

FIRST SHEPHERD

Then art thou so resolv'd? Wilt thou presume
To seek that place of death and desolation—
The ghastly kingdom of eternal night?

ORPHEUS

As the hungry infant seeks his mother's breast.

FIRST SHEPHERD

But who will show thee a way to Erebus?

ORPHEUS

Dodona's sacred groves by grace of Zeus
Will bare the way and guide my feet, e'en as
Th'oracular oak of Argo led to Colchis
Proud Jason and me and all the valiant crew.
Here in this clear stream I'll wash away
Th'effects of weak despair. The fulgent star
Begins to beam in the orient sky. The horses
Of the night do gallop fast apace,
And for the journey must I now prepare.

FIRST SHEPHERD

Then take thy leave. Father Zeus assist thee
So thy journey be not made in vain.
Farewell, my lord.

ORPHEUS

So may I thrive. Farewell.

[*Exit*]

FIRST SHEPHERD

Yet do I fear thou hastest to thy ruin;
For though I know the virtue of thy art,
All heavy with foreboding is my heart.

[*Exit. Curtain drop.*]

ACT II

Scene i

[NARRATOR *appears on apron before closed curtain.*]

NARRATOR

Deep within Dodona's oaken grove
Did Orpheus seek Pelasgic Zeus' advisement,
Nor did he seek in vain, for through his priest
Th'Olympian thus to Orpheus made reply:
"If by the stony gates of Taenarus
The Pierian bard essay to enter Dis
And to the music of his golden lyre
Will supplicate the infernal deities,
Then will his bride revivèd be; and he
A second time shall cross the Stygian flood
With her that shall be born a second time."
These honey'd words astonied so the poet
That for joy he could not speak. Thence
From dark Dodona, Orpheus on wings
Of aery hope sped southward toward Apia.
Having gain'd the promontory cliff
Of Taenarus, descried he then the cave
Whose smoky mouth, by subterranean paths
Descending, led unto the Stygian banks
Where Phoebus' darting beams did never fall.
Save for the glow of distant Phlegethon,
Darkness cover'd all.
For that the tortuous way was steep and dank,
The valiant bard, before he reach'd the plain
Of misty bogs, oft stumbled in his haste.
Full many days, O Orpheus, didst thou
Traverse th'infernal plain ere thou attainedst
Thy goal. The chill Cocytus first and next
Foul Acheron thou fordedst—rather mires
Than rivers, they. But not alone wast thou

Orpheus at the Styx

Advancing toward the city of the dead,
For on thy perilous way thou saw'st the files
Of spectres of the late interrèd dead:
Some were shades of men and women worn
With age, who moved with faltering steps; some
Were shades of those that died in greener years,
Who lightly ambled on; some hobbled by
On maimèd limbs. Some soldiers were, who bore
Fresh wounds inflicted in their cities' wars.
And some were children.

[*Pause; then curtain rises on dimly lighted stage.
Scene, the banks of the Styx. Enter* ORPHEUS *as*
NARRATOR *speaks.*]

Thus troop'd they by, this ghostly company,
And not a single footfall could be heard.
And after plodding o'er another plain
And climbing down a steep declivity,
The Pierian bard espied the watery bourn
Of Hades' empery, whereat with heart
Uplifted high thus did he speak aloud:

[*Enter* ORPHEUS.]

ORPHEUS

Behold, behold, the sombre shore of Styx!
Now my quest begins. But where in all
This noisome mist doth Charon ply his trade?

NARRATOR

There a quiet grove of osiers stand
Whose wither'd branches droop into the stream,
And to the wooded bank a shadowy form
Did loom. Seeing this, the bard exclaim'd:

ORPHEUS

'Tis even he I seek—dreaded Charon!
Lo, methinks he spies me and would speak.

[*Enter* CHARON.]

CHARON

O thou who defiest death, advance no further.
Stay thy steps. No disembodied spirit
Art thou. By thy firm and heavy footfalls
I perceive thou art a living man;
Therefore turn back from this forbidden land:
No hope survives beyond the Stygian strand.

ORPHEUS

Most fearsome is the daemon to behold.
I fain would speak to answer him, but fear
To speak, for stern and wrathful are his looks.
Now be my art as potent as my grief.

CHARON

I know not how thou hither cam'st nor why;
But mark me well, for this much do I know:
He that o'er fell Tartarus doth hold
Unbending sway hath set a soundless gulf,
Impassable, between the quick and dead;
Nor will the constant lord of darkness suffer
One of mortal kind to touch the shores
Of Erebus—not though he be king
Of all the kings that reign beneath the circle
Of the moon. All men he doth regard
With a cold and equal eye. A fool of fools
Art thou who art yet cased in mortal flesh
If thou dost think to gain the further shore.
Ere Atropos dissever thy life's thread,
Thou may'st not mongst the shades of Erebus walk,
Nor canst thou, living, hope to board my craft,
The which is wont to bear the weightless shades
And nothing more. If thou, bold man, have in thee
Aught of reason, then heed my counsel: Hence
Retrace thy steps; leave not the upper world

Again until that hour when thou shalt look
Upon thy death. Thou hast not long to wait.

NARRATOR

Orpheus at this dark counsel standeth
There aghast—like one that's caught twixt dread
And hope, and knows not whither to fly. At last
He maketh bold to utter his heart's behest:

[*Exit* NARRATOR.]

ORPHEUS

O daemon boatman, without whose needful help
The host of souls that seek their final home
Would wander through the upper world sans rest,
Sans peace, even till the end of time—
Ageless Charon, sole pilot and conductor
Of the drifting shades, to you I cry;
Yet hear my plea:
Though I am clad in mortal flesh, as you
Have mark'd, yet am I but a hollow shade;
For she that was my bride but yesterday
Doth dwell this day amongst the dead, and my heart
Abides with her whom death so lately ravish'd.
How can you number me amongst the living?
How can you truly call him living man
Who hath no heart? And so you will no law
Transgress if you would deign to grant me passage
To the kingdom of the dead.

CHARON
                    Did ever man
Embrace his ruin with such an eager will!

ORPHEUS

I pray you, mighty boatman, let me pass.
By that whereby the gods themselves do fear
To swear, by the hallow'd Styx I swear

That I would no dishonour to this realm.
I come not like some proud and rash Alcides
To disturb this quiet land of shades.

[*Arms outstretched, he approaches Charon.*]

Behold in me a wretched supplicant
That comes in peace——

CHARON
                    Hold! Approach no nearer.
Stay or perish.

[ORPHEUS *retreats several steps.*]

ORPHEUS
                    Naked and defenceless
I stand before you unarm'd save for my lyre,
Apollo's gift that sings of thwarted love,
To invocate the powers of Erebus
So they might yield to me what is my due,
So they might deign restore to me a bride
Cut off in the springtime of her life
And sever'd from my side. Though you, grave daemon,
Bear a countenance of stone, yet surely
The heart within you is wrought of softer stuff.
If that slow-dripping water can in good time
Wear away the hardest flint, then see
The tears that flow from these two stanchless founts:
Can they not find a way to reach your heart?

CHARON
Gentle poet, never before have I
Heard music like to thine. Yet know that thou
Canst rouse no pity in my breast, for there
No pity is or ever was. If heart
I had, thou wouldst ere now have melted it;
But know that I am Charon, daemon-born,
And have no heart. Thy case is otherwise.

Thou saidst thou hast no heart, for it abides
With her who was thy bride; I say thou hast—
Or ne'er couldst thou so stroke thy golden lyre.
Ah, still the music lingers in my ears.
How like some potent drug it clouds my senses
And hangs upon my lids.
[*He falls asleep.*]

ORPHEUS

      The daemon sleeps!
And even as he nods, my spirit wakes.
From the jaws of black despair the bread
Of hope has fallen pat into my hands.
Henceforth, Fortune, cursèd be the man
That calls thee false. The goddess lights my way.

[*Exit* ORPHEUS; *curtain drop.*]

Scene ii

[*Scene,* EREBUS; *enter* NARRATOR.]

NARRATOR

Now having boarded Charon's ancient craft,
Orpheus hoisted sail in the darksome mist
And glided o'er the waters of the Styx.
At last he reach'd the banks of Erebus
Upon whose chill and yielding sod he leapt
And then with wary steps resumed his quest;
But scarce an hundred paces had he walk'd
From shore when an enormous shape appear'd
Athwart his path. The bard stood still and watch'd.
There before him, stretch'd upon the ground,
Lay Cerberus, the guardian of the gates:
Cerberus, that huge three-headed beast—

Huge and fierce. Each neck with serpents teem'd,
And with each heaving breath the monster took,
Three tongues of flame leapt out three gaping jaws,
The sight whereof did reave the hero's wits.
Astonied stood he there like one half dead
As one head slowly turn'd his way and spied him.
Straightway the other two did snap about
And fix their gaze on him. And now the beast
Rear'd up, and all three heads in dreadful chorus
Howl'd. It was a strident howl and loud—
Half like the huffing roar of a furnace hot
With seething flames, half like the piercing screech
That grates the ear when iron is on iron
Scraped. Thereat the ground beneath his feet
Did quake, and cold fear smote his breast.

[*Enter* ORPHEUS.]

His lyre
He clapt unto his ribs and rais'd his fingers
To the strings. And as that hellish cur
Drew near, with fervent zeal he cried:

ORPHEUS

High Phoebus,
Aid me now in this my utmost need.
Unloose my tongue and guide my trembling hand.

NARRATOR

But ere this prayer had left his lips, the heart
Within him swell'd, setting base fear to flight.
With lighten'd hand he struck the golden strings,
And from his soul's great depths he gan to sing,
Whereat did Cerberus cease his headlong charge
And still his growls. In wonderment the beast
Uprais'd his ears; his heads in drowsiness
Then gan to nod, and one by one they sank

Upon the grass, and sweet sleep veil'd his eyes.
At the feet of Orpheus he lay.
The grateful bard, rejoicing in his heart,
Put by his lyre and thank'd the gracious giver—
Leto's son.

[*Exit* ORPHEUS *with* NARRATOR.]

Scene iii

[*Scene,* EREBUS. *Enter* NARRATOR.]

NARRATOR

Once more upon his quest the bard set out,
But soon was he beset with ghostly forms
—Thin shades that rose like vapours from the ground—
Who, seeing the shadow cast by solid flesh,
Straight knew him for a living man. Then, gliding
Through the misty air, one of these
Accosted him. In deep and spectral tones
He ask'd the poet whether he knew aught
Of his beloved spouse and son, whom he
Had left behind, but by his antique speech
Orpheus soon perceiv'd that many years
Had run their course and many wallèd towns
Had crumbled into dust long since this shade
Had walk'd the fruitful earth.
His mien was stern, and yet he look'd not proud.
Like an ancient warrior he seem'd
That in some long-forgotten battle fell.
No living man remember'd him, nor wife
Nor son; for all that knew him, now were dust:
Unknown to him, long had their spirits wander'd
Mongst those myriad swarms in that same land
Of Erebus. His name and e'en his tomb

Had time obliterated utterly.
But in that land of living death there is
No time, and so this shade knew not the folly
Of his solicitation. But Orpheus,
Sore pitying him, bespoke him fair, and said:

[*Enter* ORPHEUS *and* SPIRIT.]

ORPHEUS

Would that I could tell thee otherwise,
Good spirit, but, in truth, I know not aught
Of thy beloved spouse nor of thy son.
And yet, where'er they be, I trow that they
Do thrive and that they do remember thee.
When I regain the world of living men,
Then will I seek them out, if they yet live,
And say I spoke with thee in Erebus.

NARRATOR

After these and other gracious words
Exchanged, the spirit bow'd his head and smiled.
The bard to win his aid did thus entreat him:

ORPHEUS

Tell me, gentle spirit, if thou know,
Where in all this desolate land the Lord
Of Erebus doth keep his ghostly court?

NARRATOR

Hearing this appeal, the spirit beckon'd
Him to follow; and Orpheus, now guided
By the ancient shade, resumed his search
And saw with terror many sights full strange—
But how can my poor words describe those horrors,
Nameless and unnatural? Where, O Muses,
Where shall I begin? Though many heroes
The Gorgon's face hath straightway turn'd to stone,

What demigod is there—among those few
Who glanced thereon with some impunity—
That thought he could with words describe that face?
Alas, brave youth, as foul as fell Medusa
Or her grisly sisters were the fiends
Which thou didst see. Thrice thought he in his fear
To end his search and with celerity
Return to the world of light and flowers, alone;
But each time that these fears assaulted him,
He pictured in his mind his bride, and then
With fortified resolve defeated them.
The gods had favour'd him, and that they would
Again he doubted not, for thus he spoke:

ORPHEUS

Did not Dodonean Zeus declare that she
Would reincarnate be and I should lead her
Then across the Styx and so prevail?
The oracle doth not lie. I cannot fail.

[*Exit* ORPHEUS.]

NARRATOR

Pursued he still his goal, yet holding firm
To those dim paths whereo'er the spirit led.
And following them close behind, across the stream
Of flames that living men call *Phlegethon*
And o'er the brazen walls of Tartarus,
The screaming Furies swoop'd through the murky air,
Shaking their hideous heads as they were mad.
But notwithstanding, the poet overcame
The terrors of these final bars as he
Advancèd toward the presence of the gods.

[*Exit* NARRATOR; curtain drop.]

Scene iv

[*Tartarus.* HADES *and* PERSEPHONE *enthroned.*
Enter NARRATOR. *Enter* ORPHEUS *as* NARRATOR *speaks.*]

NARRATOR

Now did he gaze in awe upon the visage
Of great Hades: Hades, Lord of Darkness;
Hades, brother to the Thunderer.
And by his side stood tall Persephone,
Whose beauteous form illumin'd all the gloom
About her. And to these deities the bard
Made his appeal.

ORPHEUS

      Ye monarchs of this land
Whereto all mortals must one day repair,
Have mercy on a wretched man that hath
A suit with you.

HADES

      Most importunate mortal,
Report of thee hath already reach'd mine ears.
Thou art the Pierian bard clept Orpheus.
By Laconian Taenarus thou camest hither,
And by the music of thy charmèd lyre
Thou hast set thy foot upon this land
Forbidden thee. Most temerariously
Hast thou transgress'd to gain access to me;
But since that I am he thou seek'st, stand forth
And speak thy will. What wouldst thou have of Hades?

ORPHEUS

My lord, that thou wouldst give me back my bride,
Whom I do love beyond love's power to say.
Long did I woo her ere I won her love.
In a sunlit vale near Pindus we wedded were—

Near wooded Pindus, only yesterday.
But ere the garland-crownèd guests had round
The tables sat, a pall fell o'er the feast.
Their songs gave way to silence, and this the cause,
Reported by a shepherd that had in horror
Gazed upon the sight—these ears still smart
From that unlook'd-for blow:
The gracious maid, by a train of nymphs attended,
Had joyously set forth to honour Diane
In her sylvan shrine. Gathering blooms
To deck the altar stones withal, she knelt
Beside a brake, encoil'd wherein a viper
Lay. Insidiously, the furtive beast
Did sink into her foot his venom'd fangs,
Shearing away the maiden's crescent years.
Ah, how I strove to bear that heavy loss!
But though I strove amain, my grief o'erwhelm'd me.

NARRATOR

Whilst Orpheus did thus bemoan his case,
The god half turn'd from him and bow'd his head
In contemplation. And now he wheel'd about
And glarèd down upon the supplicant.
Above his temple throbb'd the azure vein,
Standing out as it would burst. His brow
Was like the gathering clouds; lightning bolted
From his eyes. A sudden wind arose
And circled round him, and like a raging sea
His locks were wildly toss'd about his head.
And when he oped his lips, there issued forth
Such fulminating words that Orpheus' ears
Thereat rang sharp.

HADES

        Handful of dust, what limit
Hath thy pride! What wilt thou next presume
To ask? Thinkest thou her life was thine?
Nay, proud man. Surely thou must know

That every mortal hath one life to live,
And she that thou dost seek hath lived the span
The Fates allotted her, albeit brief.
Whatsoe'er the Parcae bid, that let
No god gainsay, for laws divinely made
Must be observ'd. Begone. Thy cause is hopeless.

[*Enter* CHORUS *of* SPIRITS.]

NARRATOR

Shaken to his soul by this grim blast,
The poet all but yielded to despair.
He fell to silence and gazed upon the ground.

CHORUS

Yet try thy song again, thou valorous mortal.
Lift up thy lyre and try again thy song.

ORPHEUS

What shades of hell are ye that counsel hope?
You are not living men, and yet your tears
Seem almost palpable. This is most strange,
That spirits in this land should counsel hope.

CHORUS

Like thee we are but strangers to this world,
For newly sever'd are we from our clay;
And though the tears we shed are phantom tears,
They still do bid thee sing. The Orphic lyre
Is not to us unknown. When Aeson's son
And all th'intrepid Argonauts did hearken
To those sonorous melodies the Sirens
Sigh'd upon the soft Tyrrhenian zephyrs
And thereat wax'd enraptur'd, forgetting all
But those sweet strains, 'twas thou that didst deliver
Them from death: 'twas thou, by thy nobler song,
That didst o'erwhelm th'insidious sisters. Even

As thou didst save the flower of Hellas then,
So sing again and thereby redeem thy bride.
All is not hopeless.

NARRATOR

So spoke the new-come spirits. Exhorted thus,
The bard once more took up the tuneful lyre.

ORPHEUS

Too soon she died, too soon. If that her life
Should prove beyond recall, then Orpheus die!
Let Erebus exult in one more death.
If thou wilt not restore Eurydice,
Then let not Orpheus survive alone;
For we are like two beings with one heart—
Take that away, my lord, and both will die.
But if love, that holdeth sway o'er mankind,
Can with his tender suasions move the gods,
Then let him mollify thy unkind will.

HADES

What, wouldst have me countervail the laws
That govern life and death and time itself,
Call back the stars from their far-ranging orbs
And set them once again where they did stand
When she that was thy bride still walk'd the earth?
If I were Zeus, I could not do these things!
'Twere best for thee to seek thy home again.

ORPHEUS

I ask thee not to cancel time nor meddle
With the heavens, but only let her live;
For all the rest, let be. Death's lord thou art;
And, if thou wilt, her death thou canst revoke.
Did not the gentle god of love once cleave
These dense Cimmerian vapours with his darts?
Did he not even warm thy heart with love

For thy Persephone, fair queen, whom thou
Didst straight abduct from that fresh Sicilian meadow
Where the goddess was wont to sport herself
Among the flowers and round the limpid streams?
If this be true, if love thus movèd thee,
Then by him I do beseech thee: weigh
The case again and smile upon my cause.
Relinquish her at last who is my bride.
Unto the world of light and flowers restore her.

HADES

Wilful mortal, he knows not what he asks.

PERSEPHONE

Nay, hear him, my lord. I cannot choose but weep
To think how much this noble mortal dares—
And all for love of her that was his bride.
He moves me much. For my sake hear his plea.

HADES

Well, I will hear him, but 'tis to no avail.

ORPHEUS

What is it that I seek so stirs thy wrath?—
A brief reprieve for one untimely slain.
And what are these few years to thee? Will not
The shade of her I love be thine at last?
What difference if tomorrow or today?
The life of mortals passes in a wink,
But eternity is long.

NARRATOR

The bloodless spirits wept for him whilst he
Was speaking thus, stroking the dulcet strings.
Thereat did Tantalus forget his thirst
And cease to catch at the falling flood. And now
Ixion's wheel, though senseless stone, halted

And fell ponderous to the ground. And thou,
O weary Sisyphus, amazèd sat
Upon thy rock. Then did the ravenous vultures
Stint in rending from Tityus' bleeding side
The liver; and as they perch'd there stunn'd, a froth
Of blood and gore dripp'd from their loathsome beaks.
And the Belides, setting aside their urns,
Did cease their fruitless toil. It was a wonder
How his music moved the murky region,
Shedding light where there was naught before
But moaning and impenetrable gloom.
'Tis even said th'Eumenides did weep
To hear him sing—the wild Eumenides,
Whose wither'd cheeks ne'er felt till then one drop
Of pity. But more than they and all the host
Of shades was fair Persephone now moved
To warm compassion. Turning to her lord,
The gentle goddess thus entreated him:

PERSEPHONE

Amaz'd, I stare upon this creature's ruin
And my soul resolves herself to tears.
What! shall th'Erinyes be movèd and not thou?
Shall gods and men say Hades hath no mercy?
Or doth imperious pride decree that thou
Must to thy primal judgement hold? Ah, gods
Have err'd before and shall again. If thou
Wouldst rather let the poet perish here
Than yield to his appeal, disdain not then
The imploration of a tongue divine:
My lord, if thou didst ever love me, free
The maid. Restore her to her loving spouse.
Pray, my lord, do not deny me this.

NARRATOR

These words she spoke as if her heart would break.
What fortress would not yield to such a siege?
When Orpheus had batter'd down the gates,

Persephone did storm the citadel.
Then gazing tenderly upon his queen,
Hades heav'd a sigh and said to her:

HADES

Leave thy weeping and wringing of thy hands
Or thou wilt, like Pirene, turn to water.
Granted is thy wish. Yet do I fear
The Fates will not concur.

NARRATOR
Turning next
To Orpheus, the lord of darkness spoke.

HADES

Thus far thou hast prevail'd. Now hear my doom,
Thou poet of the golden lyre: Hereby
Do I grant thy hotly press'd petition.
Ay, thou mayest have thy bride and lead her
Safely to the world of light and flowers.
But one condition must thou yet fulfill——

ORPHEUS

Any condition! so be it in my power.
Any condition thou wilt say, my lord.

HADES

Then list thee well to what I have to say.
When thou shalt pass beyond the Avernian vales,
Departing from my dark dominion, then
Thou mayest turn about and look behind thee
And there behold thy bride; but ere those vales
Thou have travers'd, forbear to look upon her,
Nor aught of discourse hold with her—this is
My doom, and hold it well within thy heart,
For if thou keep not this condition, then leave
All hope behind thee. There is no more to say.

NARRATOR

As the stout-arm'd woodman that labours hard
Throughout the sunlit hours along the sea-coast
Of Thassalia, felling one great oak
And then another, until his shoulder scarce
Upholds the burden of the axe, turneth
To a promontory, and there doth feel
A cool and gusty wind embrace his brow:
Even so did Orpheus now feel
These soothing words uplift his torpid heart.
He then bethought himself how all his hopes
Were now fulfill'd, and with o'erbrimming gladness
Thus address'd he Hades:

ORPHEUS

All honour and glory attend thy ageless reign,
Most mighty god. Know ye, Tartarean powers,
That Orpheus will never cease to sing
Of Hades' matchless magnanimity
And the loving mercy of his gracious queen
To all the world. O lead me to my bride!

[*Exit* NARRATOR, *then* HADES *and* PERSEPHONE *with*
ORPHEUS. CHORUS *remains.*]

CHORUS

Why art thou sad, O man of little faith?
Why wanderest thou in darkness, lone and trembling?
By Orpheus' example know thee well
The gods are just and merciful to man.
Be thou not therefore dismay'd, but trust thee
In the gods and cast from thee forthwith
Thy mantle of leaden doubts. And lifting high
Thy spirit, look with piety on them
That look on thee with love.

[*Exit* CHORUS, *curtain drop.*]

ACT III

[*Scene, the same. Enter* NARRATOR.]

NARRATOR

The sovereign lord of death now rais'd his right hand,
And a shaft of thunder straightway clove the darkness
And made the neighbour ground to shake beneath him.
Anon a second bolt did smite the earth
And rend it wide, from out whose smoking rift
A tongue of purple flame arose, the which
Bedazzled so the poet's eyes that, turning,
Orpheus gazed not on't, but hid his face
Between his hands. In a swirling, silver mist
Eurydice now appear'd. And as a cloud,
A wispy cloud, doth veil bright Phoebe's face
And with a glowing aura crowns her brow,
So the maiden in her nuptial gown
Resplendent stood before him. Mounting bliss
O'erreaching mortal measure swell'd his breast
So that for joy he wept. Anon the bard
Stood still, mindful of Hades' stern decree,
And look'd not on his bride, but let his heart
In silence burn. Yet to himself he spoke.

ORPHEUS

Now could boundless joy my passion crown,
But that a strange, uneasy sadness lieth
Next my heart. I know not whence it comes.
What desolation doth my soul presage?
Nay, none. What, must I frown when Fortune smiles?
Superfluous joy will not be contain'd;
And even as the excess overflows,
It troubles me and cheers me all at once.
Not unalloy'd comes unaccustom'd joy;
Hence, men that have been stretch'd on Fortune's rack
Will not smile easily when they're unbound.

What cause have I to doubt? Why, none at all.
Now can I scent the sweetness of her presence,
Though I dare not with mine eyes avouch it;
And were she not enjoin'd to present silence,
Then would she speak. I long to hear her voice;
Yet will I bide.

NARRATOR

Thus to himself he spoke.
And once again he put aside his fears
And pale misgiving. Under Hades' aegis
The bard retraced his way secure—once more
Across the fiery stream and past the beast
That keeps the gates, and with him went his bride.
Through the land of living death he walk'd,
And she with halting steps did follow him
For that her foot still bore a healing wound.
With grudging will the daemon ferried them
Across the Styx, indignant still with him
That had so lull'd his wits and stol'n his bark.
And in that desolate land beyond the Styx
The bard, with heavy limbs but lightened heart,
Still plied his homeward course.
But soon his apprehensive doubts return'd:
Like straggler crows that slowly flock together,
They drifted one by one before his eyes,
Making dark the path that lay before him.
The more he near'd his goal, the more he fear'd
That when at last he gain'd the upper world
And turn'd to look upon Eurydice,
Then she would not be there.
Perhaps th'infernal god did perpetrate
Some monstrous ruse, he thought—or that, tiring,
She had falter'd far behind. He scarce
Could quell these goading doubts, and ere he reach'd
Avernus, he stay'd his steps and look'd behind him.
And there he saw his bride—as fresh and fair
As when she woke upon her wedding day.

[*Here he pauses.*]
Now Fortune doth her tragic curtain draw.
As when Narcissus spied his mirror'd image
In the argent brook, and, being seiz'd
Thereby with drunken desire, did thrust his arms
Into the flood as if he would embrace
Th'incorporal object of his bootless love,
And as that image, midst the ripples trembling,
Vanish'd from his ken, and naught but water
Did the forlorn lover clasp: E'en so
Did Orpheus, in stretching forth his arms
To clasp his bride withal, behold her melt
Into the Cimmerian mist—even there
Before his eyes; nor did he touch her, but clutch'd
At naught but the yielding wind. Dying thus
A second death, she bade her last farewell,
The which did barely touch her lover's ear;
And yet her eyes wore no impugning look
And not a word of blame escaped her lips,
For whereof could the hapless bride complain,
But that she was loved? When a hyacinth,
His petall'd head turn'd upward to the sun,
Is rudely trod on by a wanton beast,
The bruisèd stem no longer bears the burden
Of his own dishevell'd top: for lo,
Wind-toss'd it nods, first one way, then another,
Till the stem doth cease his vain support,
And the purple bloom—now leaning on his stem—
Doth stare upon the ground. Even as such
A ruin'd flower, Orpheus' fair head
Now falls upon his breast.

[CHORUS *appears upstage right, behind scrim, elevated
and softly lighted. Enter* ORPHEUS *from left.*]

CHORUS
Who can lend thee comfort now?
Who can calm thy breast?

Can all the heavens not give thee peace
Nor lend thee one moment's rest?

ORPHEUS

What, art thou gone, Eurydice? Is it
For this that I prevail'd against the gates
Of Tartarus? In vain have I endured
The abominable horrors of that place?
What hope remains? Sooner will high Ossa
On stormy Pelion be piled than I
Redeem my bride again. Lo, Orpheus,
Where are thy rosy dreams since hope hath fled,
Abandoning thee in thy most desperate need?
How dost thou reckon Fortune now, ha?—thou
Who hast won a second turn about her wheel?
And only yesterday thou saidst to her,
"Cursèd be the man that calls thee false."
Now art thou curst indeed. Twice she rais'd thee
High, and twice she cast thee down; nor shalt
Thou rise again. Divine Executrix,
How lovingly didst thou once pamper me!
Thou false dissembler, I took thee for a friend.
The perfidious goddess ever maketh fat
Her witless gulls ere she doth slaughter them.
He that calls the gods benevolent
Is but a reverent gull or else a liar;
For they deceivèd me, even they,
The prescient deities that men call just,
For ever is't their pleasure to deceive
Mankind—it cannot truly be denied.
They saw the end and yet abetted me,
Knowing that thereby they would destroy me.

CHORUS

Who can lend thee comfort now?
Who can give thee rest?

ORPHEUS

But hold. What blasphemy is this! Nay, why

'Gainst Fortune and the gods do I now rail?
Debilitating grief assaileth me strong,
And I do think amiss. From minds oppress'd
With sorrow, full many wayward thoughts may rise
To confound reason. But see these falling tears—
Methinks they would proclaim where lies the guilt.
'Tis in mine eyes! mine own accursèd eyes—
And that frail will which made those ministers
Of folly look upon her all too soon.
Irrevocable error. Doubting she
Did follow close behind me and longing so
To see her face again, I turn'd to look;
And, looking, I did slay her where she stood—
Ay, as surely as I had plunged a dagger
In her throat. Damnèd, damnèd eyes!
That I should play the cockatrice and kill her
With a glance! Would that I had died
So thou mightest live, sweet maid, so thou mightest live.
Now could I thrust my fingers in my eyes
And pluck the rooted eyeballs from my head
And weep away this life with tears of blood.
That I the blessed gods did execrate
I am ashamed. In truth, the architect
Of his own fate is man. The choice is his;
And if he choose amiss, he cannot justly
Blame the gods. The fault is his alone.
Fortune favours not the injudicious.
Dead thou art, my fair Eurydice,
And Orpheus is thy wretched murderer.
He that loved thee most did slay thee. Behold,
The Avernian gate! But one bare moment longer.
O that I my fatal doubts had held
In reign one moment longer! Too late. Too late.

CHORUS

Who can lend thee comfort now?
Who can calm thy breast?
The heavens cannot give thee peace
Nor lend thee one moment's rest.

ORPHEUS

That I the god's condition would abide
I swore most solemnly. "Any condition
Thou wilt say, so be it in my power."
Thus did I speak and thus am I forsworn,
False to my love and faithless to the gods.
Through my art I dared more than a god,
Yet am I less than a man.

LEADER OF THE CHORUS

Alas, poor creature, thou hast conquer'd Hades
Only to be vanquish'd by thyself.

NARRATOR

Aimlessly wandering, the dazèd bard
Did haunt the place where she had vanish'd, as if
She would appear again, until at last
Returning to the Stygian stream, he broke
The silence of the dead and shouted loud,
His wounded heart rising in his throat
As if to choke him.

ORPHEUS

        Black depths of Tartarus,
Give me back my bride! Hades, Hades,
Hear me once again. Forgive my fault
And let her live again. Answer me!
When wilt thou answer me?

NARRATOR

The faintest echoes from th'opposing bank
Did mock his anxious cries. With downcast gaze
He still'd his tongue and sat there in deep dejection,
Alone within the ear-oppressing silence
Of that vast and lifeless void. Nothing
Could he descry except the drifting shades,
More numerous than the wither'd leaves of autumn

Strown thick on windy slopes of Appenine
As far as eye can see.

CHORUS

Orpheus,
Let words now yield to tears, tears to despair—
Despair that vulture-like doth gnaw thy vitals,
Leaving thee but a torn and empty shell.
No longer are we strangers to this land;
We see at last the perpetual night of hell.

[*Extinguish scrim lights, then exit* CHORUS.]

NARRATOR

Thrice did Phoebus wend his wonted course
Whilst Orpheus sat upon the Styx' black brim;
Nor did he aught of Ceres' presents taste,
But ate the bread of grief and vain remorse.
Her second death a second time he mourn'd,
But now his grief was twofold: Before, his sorrow
Had a tongue; now, within him stopt,
It burn'd the more. Before, he upright stood
And weeping loud he told his heavy care
To all the world; now sits he tearless, speechless,
All benumb'd.
There gan he make a mirror of his mind,
Wherein the lively image of his love
He saw—as she did seem when first he look'd
Upon her blushing face: a tender maiden,
Beauty's bloom, even in the April
Of her life. But these fair thoughts, alas,
Did only send fresh streams of torment pouring
Into grief's o'erflowing cup. How dreams
Of former bliss do pain the anguish'd soul!
Soon turn'd he from his mind these futile thoughts,
For in his heart he knew full well his bride
He would behold no more. The bargain broke,

There was no cure. Thus sat he there in darkness,
Like a stone; and no sound pierced the gloom,
Save for the moans of the countless shades that dwell
Along the further shore. Hollow-sounding,
Like the winds that blow from snowy Pindus,
Was the murmur of that phantom host.
And on the third day he put away his silence
With a heavy sigh and spake these words:

ORPHEUS

Ah, empty heart, ere this thou shouldst have broken.
To whom shall I make my supplication? To me
The gods are deaf. They will not hear. O Death,
Thou mighty sunderer, I that rail'd on thee
Would call thee father if thou wouldst lift me up
And clasp me to thy bosom. See, dread lord,
How willingly I now could make an end
To this most bitter and untenable life.
Or else in Lethe's waters might I bathe
And wash my every memory away;
Then should I purge my mind of this remorse,
This endless anguish that renders life more dread
Than ghastly death. There were a cleansing indeed!
[a pause]
But what fond thoughts are these? Spare atonement
Would either prove for wrongs as grave as mine.
Is't just that I by death should 'scape remorse?
Or is it just that I should bide in peace,
Forgetful of my fault, while she doth wander
Through the land of shadows? Nay. 'Tis meet
That I abide this mortal course and so
Remember her, and with each new remembrance
Die another death.

NARRATOR

To brooding silence fell he once again,
And no sound pierced the gloom, save for the moans
Of the shades that dwell along the further shore.

[*As* NARRATOR *speaks the following lines,* ORPHEUS *rises, crosses right, and exits.*]

Anon, from his sedentary state he rose,
Turning his back upon dark Erebus,
And wearily made his way to the upper world,
Leaving behind the somber world of shadows.
Then saw he once again the light of heaven,
Which he had thought he would behold no more;
And yet that light of heaven, warm and glowing,
Held no joy for him, nor did the flowers
Of the field, nor the purling mountain streams—
Surveying all these wonders, he saw how they
Delighted him not.

[*As* NARRATOR *continues, enter* ORPHEUS *behind scrim back-lighted in rose-tinted glow of sunset. Appearing in silhouette, he climbs rocky eminence. Light is gradually dimmed.*]

        Then westward to the sea-shore
Orpheus wander'd—west, among the tall pines
That raise the verdure of their spreading crowns
Above the rich Campanian plain. And there
He scaled a craggy promontory that juts
High o'er the Tuscan surf. And lifting up
His lyre, which glitter'd golden in the sun—
The dying sun whose beams, now falling, dipt
Into the distant wave—he hurl'd it down
Into the swirling foam and stood there, scanning
The far horizon: a solitary figure
Against the vasty sky. And thus he stood,
Motionless and hush, till out of the east
The billowy darkness roll'd upon the earth.

[*Curtain drop*]

Prometheus Unvanquished

PREFACE

In adapting the Promethean myth to my purposes, I have in a sense interposed a fourth play between two plays of Aeschylus' epic trilogy: *Prometheus Bound* and the sequent play, the lost *Prometheus Unbound*. There is no universal agreement about whether the lost *Prometheus the Fire-bearer (Prometheus Luomenos)* is the first or the last play of the trilogy. Since, in either case, the last play has not survived, the precise manner in which Aeschylus resolved the reconciliation of Zeus and Prometheus remains uncertain. In his dramatic poem *Prometheus Unbound*, Shelley departs from the Aeschylan version by rejecting the reconciliation in favor of the deposition of Jupiter by Demogorgon, an event that occurs before Hercules liberates Prometheus. I have elected to follow Aeschylus' design, as far as it may be reconstructed from extant fragments, to the extent that in my play Prometheus prophesies the reconciliation, which is in part mediated by Heracles.

I have chosen to simplify the action by omitting reference to Io and the Oceanides, the inclusion of which would have introduced complications better suited to a longer play. What the play has thereby lost in complexity and scope it has perhaps gained in clarity and concision.

There are Christ-like traits in both the Prometheus of Aeschylus and of Shelley, and in the works of both authors, especially Shelley's, Zeus/Jupiter is tyrannical. In the grandeur of his rebellious pride there is also, as the poet notes in his preface, something of Milton's Satan in Shelley's hero. The Titan of *Prometheus Unvanquished* remains both a Christ-like hero and a proud rebel; however, though Prometheus is the hero of the play, the center of sympathy shifts appreciably toward Zeus, who may be right, after all, in judging that man is ultimately incapable of employing the forbidden knowledge wisely and that consequently the divine fire will in the end destroy him. In *Prometheus Unvanquished,* as in Aeschylus' play, there is right and wrong on both sides.

Zeus is a jealous god, for there is in him not a little of the Old Testament Jaweh. He represents divine order and authority, but is nevertheless an arbitrary tyrant whose judgment and whose sense of justice are suspect. In great dudgeon he says to Prometheus:

> Knowest thou not that what I will is just,
> And justice is whate'er I will? . . .

Prometheus represents free will, reason, and mercy toward mankind, but he is not entirely free of *hubris*. The Heracles of Prometheus' prophecy is Christ-like in that he is both man and god and in that he reconciles man and god (viz., Zeus, his divine father).

It is sometimes assumed that a Promethean drama must necessarily be static inasmuch as its hero, bound to a rock, is the center of the action—a critical view that might have some validity if the play were to be presented in the form of a dumb-show or a silent cinema. In *Prometheus Unvanquished* the dramatic action is contained in the dialogue, which is doubtless of greater moment than mere physical movement from place to place.

It can be disconcerting to see the intrusive and pointless stage business that often mars current productions of Classical or Elizabethan plays. Frank O'Connor, the author-poet who directed plays at the Abbey Theatre in its early years, said:

> I saw Yeats' original production of his own
> translation of *Oedipus Rex,* in which Oedipus

hardly changed his position . . . and for once I wanted to scream. Years later I saw Laurence Olivier's production of the same version, and Laurence, remembering that "Oedipus" means "clubfoot," demonstrated the fact by jumping up and down boxes until I wanted to cry: "Is there an orthopedic surgeon in the house." That, it seems to me, is the weakness of the Shakespearean convention; it runs to irrelevant bits of business that merely distracts attention from the eternal words.[1]

Spectacle—both scenery, lighting, and blocking—is an integral part of a play as long as it does not distract the audience from the dialogue, the *eternal words*. It was not simply a matter of idiom when Elizabethans said that they were going "to hear" a play.

The dialogue of *Prometheus Unvanquished* is concentrated in a clash of wills—in the stupendous conflict between Zeus and Prometheus, both of whom act out of stubborn conviction. In style I have striven to emphasize the dramatic and the epic, employing diction, schemes, tropes, and devices of prosody to produce something of the epic clarity, strength, and dignity necessary to sustain the contention of gods against a cosmic setting. The heightening of language is, I believe, essential in this epic drama since it would be absurd for immortal gods to speak the language of men. I am, of course, quite aware of the narrow path one must tread in order to succeed at such a task as this. On the one hand one risks turgidity and on the other a pedestrianism that is, if anything, worse. I hope that I have avoided both.

The themes of the play, the duality of man's nature and the problem of free will vs. divine order, are universal and require no comment here. At any rate, a play should be able to speak for itself.

---

1. Frank O'Connor, *My Father's Son* (1968; rpt. London: Pan Books, 1971), p. 154.

Prometheus Unvanquished

DRAMATIS PERSONAE

SPIRIT

CHORUS OF MEN

PROMETHEUS

HERMES

ZEUS

Prometheus Bound

Scene i

[*The curtain rises on an empty stage, dimly lighted. Scene: the Caucasus. Time: the Bronze Age; early morning, before dawn. Mountain peaks are silhouetted against a cyclorama, the black sky filled with stars. The light brightens perceptibly, revealing snow and a rocky terrain as* SPIRIT, *clad in a long black robe, enters down stage right. He walks slowly to right centre and looks off right. As* CHORUS *enters from stage left,* SPIRIT *speaks.*]

SPIRIT

Who trespasses upon this sacred ground?
Why come ye here to this cold and cheerless region
Where no man dwells and only the passing eagle
Sometimes soars?

CHORUS

We are the sons of man.
Our home is on a distant Attic shore
From whence we sail'd across the broad Aegean
In a deep-hull'd ship, past narrow Hellespont,
Propontis, and o'er the wine-dark Euxine Sea;
And to this wild and mountainous land we come
To mourn for him that suffers for our sake.
Where is the noble god?

SPIRIT

Now have ye compass'd full your journey's goal:
The ageless Titan that ye seek is near.
Lift up your eyes to yonder peak and see

Against the myriad stars his stalwart form
Forwrapt in clouds that coil in billows round him.

[*It is to be imagined that* PROMETHEUS, *as if visible only to
the actors on stage, is above and off stage right.*]

CHORUS

O vast and beauteous god, 'tis truly thou,
Creator and conserver of mankind.
Long have we search'd for thee, and now great sorrow
It causeth us to see thee. Would that we
Were Titans and not men, that we might thee
Deliver from thy endless pain and set thee
Free. But we are frail and puny mortals,
And we can only gaze on thee and weep:
Tears, bootless tears!—small recompense,
Prometheus, for all thou gavest us.
See how his head inclines upon his breast
And his flowing locks half veil his countenance.
How many years has he suffer'd thus?

SPIRIT

Nay, ask how many ages.

CHORUS

Alas, th'Olympian's wrath is boundless then.
How came he to be chain'd upon this peak?
What direful punishment did Zeus devise?
Recount the woeful tale, for we would know,
That we our debt to him might comprehend.

SPIRIT

Great indeed is your debt to him that bore
To earth the sacred fire. When that the son
Of Clymene, disdaining Zeus' decree,
Secreted in a hollow staff the flame
He stole and proffer'd it to humankind
For their enlightenment, the Thunderer,

With Power standing at his side, did stun
The Titan with a bolt and hurl him earthward.
Then bade he strong Hephaestus bind him here.
And to this craggy peak tied fast were his limbs,
And the frigid chains press'd hard against his breast.
About him raged a rushing storm of wind.
Sun-searèd were his eyes: he scarce could see.
Anon, at Zeus' command, the dreadful lord
Of lofty crests and slopes from aery clouds
Swoop'd down and perch'd upon the helpless Titan.
With talons in Prometheus' thigh deep-dug,
The ravenous eagle spread his pinions wide,
Embow'd his neck, and, darting fast his beak,
Did rend his victim's side.
Into the raging wound he thrust his head
And gan to gorge upon th'exposèd liver.
All down Prometheus' right side ran the blood
That well'd from out the wound. His grisly feast
Now ended, Zeus' fell beast stretch'd forth his neck,
And from his throat there came a piercing shriek
That echo'd round the region. Flying aloft,
He left his writhing host. Ah, who could look
Upon the noble god and not be moved
To pity! When Night let fall her sable cloak
Upon the rugged back of Caucasus,
The flow of blood did ebb, then cease; the wound
Began to mend; and, deep within the side
Of this immortal Titan, the ravaged liver
Grew whole again, and he felt his strength return.
But soon his immortality he rued;
For, on the morrow, when in his prime bright Phoebus
Stood, then did the stricken god descry
Against the rack a darkling, distant form
Descend in circles. Once more the piercing cry
He heard, and saw once more the looming beast.
Alas, what more is there to say? Must I
Again anatomize the agony
Of this fair god? Must I again recall

To mind how he did vainly strive to burst
His bonds until he thought his heart would burst?—
How every day the eagle tore his side,
And every night his wounds would mended be?
Prometheus, Prometheus, the ocean
Of dark anguish thou alone hast fathom'd.
For man's sake thou hast suffer'd grievous pain—
For man, that feeble creature of a day,
Whom thou dost love, and whom thou didst save.

CHORUS

It hath scor'd our hearts to hear thee speak.
What power is there in all the universe
Can stand against the will of Cronus' son?
To him we raise our arms in supplication.
To him we cry. O royal Zeus, who speakest
With the voice of wide-resounding thunder,
Whose kingdom is the boundless universe,
If ever thou hast found our sacrifices
Pleasing to thine eyes, then hear our prayer.
Have mercy on him who steadfast stood by thee
Gainst that Titanic mutiny which shook
Thy royal throne. We beseech thee, Lord,
Relent thy wrath, recall thy awful doom,
And free Prometheus from his agony.

[*Curtain drop*]

Scene ii

[*Scene, the same; time, later the same morning. A light wind.*
PROMETHEUS *at stage left centre, naked and bound to a huge
rock. On his right side a large wound partly visible; smaller
wounds on his thighs. For a time he remains silent and
motionless, like a statue; then, slowly, he raises his head and
speaks.*]

PROMETHEUS

The tempering winds of time inure me not.
Hard custom hath not dull'd the edge of pain.
Burst, clouds, your smoky seams and weep. Weep
Away your burden in a flood of tears,
And drench my burning head and soothe my limbs—
My smarting limbs and side. How every atom
Of my being in anguish cries! And yet,
For all the pain, no mercy will I beg
Of Cronus' son. Never will I bend.

[*Off stage*]

HERMES

Prometheus!

PROMETHEUS

Who calls my name? Be thou god or man,
Stand forth and reveal thyself!
                    [*Aside*]   My lips are sere.
I cannot speak but they do crack and bleed.

[*Enter* IIERMES.]

HERMES

Thou dost know me well. Hermes am I—
Fleet messenger of Zeus. It sore aggrieves me
To see thee here, a fellow god, thus bound
In misery upon this barren rock.
How great a fall was thine, Prometheus!
High Zeus, Olympus' king, was wont to seek
Thy counsel ere thy fall, for he thy prescience
Well esteem'd. When thou didst him forwarn
Against thy brother Titans' rude assault,
He well did heed thy words and set about
To marshal his immortal host and foil
Th'intended siege. And when that mighty throng

Gan storm the gates, the ireful Zeus his host
Led forth in sally and shock'd the Titan centre.
The powers, equal match'd, held fast the whiles.
In doubt the issue stood as in the heavens
Wingèd Nike held her golden scales
Counterpois'd between the warring hosts.

PROMETHEUS

Full well do I recall that dreadful day.
The blood-red sky resounded loud with clash
Of coruscating arms as god struck god.
The earth below did shake, and vast Olympus
Groan'd upon his base. When gods make war,
The elements themselves do jar; for then
A thousand tempests did convulse the sky,
The seas in fury boil'd, and mounting waves
Did rush upon the land to drown the shores
And batter gainst her craggy sentinels.
If order and degree were then o'erthrown,
Creation into chaos had dissolv'd,
Whence it had erst been fashion'd by the gods.
Thus did the universe imperill'd stand
Until at last the Titan power falter'd,
And Zeus with bolts of flashing thunder smote
The routed ranks. Into the deepest pit
Of Tartarus he flung the Titans down.

HERMES

Full sweet and glorious was the victory
Wherein thou didst an ample share enjoy.
Then unto heaven and earth came Peace. She came
Like a gracious breath from Tempe in the spring,
And the mansions of the blessed rang with laughter.
Dear to Zeus and all the regnant gods
Wast thou, Prometheus. Wherefore, then,
Didst set thy heart gainst Zeus and lightly forfeit
Thy exalted station? Didst think thyself
Too lordly to be bound by his decrees?
Or didst thou so love humankind to welcome

Thy own ruin? Where was thy prescient art
When thou didst flout thy lord? Oh, rash Titan—
To be so wholly blinded by thy pride!

PROMETHEUS

I'll hear no more.
Hence, false lackey! Thou hast come to mock me.

HERMES

Nay. I come to thee at Zeus' behest
To cheer thy desolate heart with joyful news.
Raise thy haggard head and hear my words.

PROMETHEUS

What guileful noise wilt thou regurgitate?
What vipers now hath Zeus his vengeance spawn'd!

HERMES

Through no desert of thine, Zeus doth extend
To thee his grace. With humbled heart accept it,
And thou wilt be unbound, and thou wilt suffer
Pain no more. Thus Zeus did bid me speak,
And I, obedient to his sovereign will,
Report his words aright to thee. And yet,
For all I care, thou surly Titan, I would
That thou wert doubly bound! But here advanceth
The lord of all the universe himself.
He strides among the stars. Thou wilt behold him
Ere this golden light of heaven wane.
If thou have any grain of judgement left,
Thou wilt receive him graciously; or else
Precedent torment shall but a prologue prove
To that which follows. I'll speak with thee no more.

[*Exit* HERMES.]

PROMETHEUS

Well, let him come. Who can hinder Zeus
Or turn him from the course of his fix'd purpose?

[*Curtain drop*]

Scene iii

[Scene, the same; time, dusk of the same day. The stage is lighted in the ruddy glow of dusk. As the scene progresses and twilight yields to night, PROMETHEUS *is seen against a cyclorama of stars, which gradually increase their number and brightness. As the stage grows darker, a spot of light, like an aura, illuminates* PROMETHEUS *and by degrees becomes brighter, particularly toward the end of his last speech.]*

PROMETHEUS

The darkness spreads apace across the land,
And yet I have not seen the harrowing beast
That doth each day unseam my wounds again.
Ne'er since the hour I to this rock was bound
Have I not felt his sting within my bowels.
I scann'd the racking clouds and spied him not.
If Zeus relent betimes, then have I err'd.
Behold the pendent stars increase their light:
The day is almost agone, and Zeus will come.
What doth it bode? Am I Prometheus still
And cannot see what yet will come to pass?

[A peal of thunder. Enter ZEUS.*]*

ZEUS

Attend me well. Know thou, wretched god,
That 'tis for thy sake I do come to thee
From out of my celestial sphere. For that
Thou didst commit grave treason gainst thy lord,
I causèd thee to suffer grievous pain
For thrice a thousand years. Gods and men
Must know that Zeus' decrees, not lightly made,
May not be lightly broken. Prometheus,
To think on thee it maketh me sad. Fair Titan,
I had hoped to share with thee some portion
Of my majesty, for I did love thee

Well. But thou didst cruelly me betray.
From Olympus thou didst steal forbidden fire,
The which, in bold defiance of my will,
Thou gavest to mankind. Forasmuch
As I perceiv'd that men were too unwise,
That element from them I did withhold.

PROMETHEUS

And therein didst thou err, for ever men
Increase in wisdom. To their own devices
Leave them, and surely thou wilt see them pluck
From Nature's breast her hid and secret laws.
They have in them a smatch of deity.

ZEUS

Nay, Prometheus, Zeus doth not err.
This mortal race engender'd is of clay,
And therefore needs must be to earth confin'd.
Albeit true that when the mortal lives
Of men be spent, their shades survive to drift
About the murky halls of death, yet these
Are only earthbound wraiths that smell of clay.

PROMETHEUS

Ay, men are less than gods; yet still are they
Akin to gods. And if their blasted shades
Were free from out their subterranean vaults
To rise into the purer air, then thou
Wouldst see them blossom forth a nobler breed.

ZEUS

Nay, Prometheus. Believe it not.
The fullness of time will prove I judg'd aright.
Trust me. How have these mortals used thy gift?
Behold thy handiwork and see how beastly
Men do live. And yet in all the world
There was no creature happier than man.

He thirsted not for gold, nor sought he fame;
The fruitful earth supplied his every need.
He cared not to enlarge his fair dominion;
With bloody war the beauty of his fields
Was then unmarr'd. But thou wast not content
To leave him thus in peace and innocence.
The fire that seemingly augments the state
Of man and in his soul, divine ambition
Kindles—did germinate within that soul
Corrosive seeds of lust; and ever since
Hath anxious Care sat brooding on his breast.

PROMETHEUS

Man walks upright and looks toward the stars,
And so he did before I gave him fire.
Not forever would he bide the darkness:
In blind simplicity he scorn'd to stay,
Despite his natural imperfections. And now
Man oft o'erreaches his exiguous powers,
So high doth wit his proud ambition spur.
That thus far-searching knowledge bringeth care,
It cannot be denied; but surely man
Is worthy of a nobler portion, O Zeus,
Than to lie content in sloughs of ignorance.
The universe of cold and thoughtless matter
Is but an atom to the mind of man.

ZEUS

That thou, renown'd for wisdom mongst the gods,
Shouldst be in this sole case bereft of reason!
Remember how another god, like thee,
Prometheus, in majesty and might,
Did grossly err in magnifying man.
When Phaethon, Phoebus' mortal son, presumed
In his vainglory to race the solar car
Across the field of day, the fiery steeds
Against his unskill'd hand rebell'd and ran
A wild, eccentric course. So near the earth

They ran that forthwith all the world in flames
Had perish'd. But with a thunderbolt I smote
The terror-frozen youth and dash'd him headlong
To the ground. In wisdom Phoebus is
Not least among the gods; but fond affection
Ever blindeth wit, and therefore did
The doting god his sacred charge deliver
Into the hands of his audacious son.
As Phaethon fell to earth, so shall mankind.
The fire thou didst contrive to steal and give
To man will in the end destroy him, nor leave
Behind a smoking cinder; and therefore all
In vain have been thy labours for mankind,
And thy agony also. But let us set
Aside our ancient quarrel. I come to thee
In peace. The floodtide of my wrath has pass'd,
And soft compassion rules my breast. And Zeus
Hath not forgot thy former constancy—
When thou didst stoutly shield my majesty
Against the Titans' mutinous assault.
Enough hast thou endured. And now Hephaestus
Will I summon, and I will bid him burst
The bonds of adamant that long have held thee
Fast upon this mountain.

PROMETHEUS

Is't even so? May I believe it?

ZEUS

Yea, Prometheus. Though I may seem
To thee a judge too fix'd and stern, yet know,
Proud Titan, that Zeus is not unmerciful.
O doubt me not, but with a credent ear
Attend my words. It is my sovereign will
That thou shouldst straightway be unbound. I say
Thou shalt be free and so shalt e'er remain,
If thou wilt but amend thy rebellious mind.
Let there at last be peace and love betwixt us.

Thy ancient sin acknowledge and never more
Make bold to judge thy lord, but let thy will
Conform to mine. Thy bootless contumacy
Thou must renounce, submitting to me in all things—
And hereby thou wilt reap thy freedom.

PROMETHEUS

                             Freedom?
Thou wouldst unbind my limbs and bind my will,
And this thou callest freedom!
Now, insidious god, I spy thy purpose.
I did suspect thy proffer'd amnesty
Would bear a heavy price. Well, I like
It not. Rather would I be Prometheus
Bound and master of my will than be
Prometheus unbound and made a slave,
An abject slave that lives to flatter Zeus.

ZEUS

None may with impunity defy me,
Whatever be the pretext or the cause!
Through contravention of my sovereign will,
Thou broughtest on thy own head my lawful wrath.
It doth avail thee naught to thus persist
In surquedry and obstinate contention
Gainst thy lord omnipotent. Thou art
Foredoom'd to fail. Why wilt thou not accept
These light conditions to an amnesty?

PROMETHEUS

A guiltless mortal that is falsely judg'd
And bears for two years' time the iron burden
Of his chains doth not, when he's releas'd
Therefrom, burst forth in giddy exultation;
But toward the sullen earth he bends to rub
His gallèd ankles and mutely curse the chains
That held him close whilst he with staring eyes

O'erwatch'd the file of months creep slowly by him.
And if this manumitted prisoner
Would thus contemn his momentary bondage,
What must I do if I should be unbound?—
I that have at thy unjust command
These aeons suffer'd sharp, abiding pain!
With what asperity this indignation
Rankles in my breast! Imperious god,
Must I then kneel and clasp thy sacred knees
And say, "O Zeus, I thank thee for thy mercy.
By thy munificence dost thou now open
Wide my heart, and therein I behold
At last such monstrous culpability
That I am smitten with remorse"? Is't thus
That thou wouldst have me whimper? Nay, proud god,
This I will not do. If thou, with all
Thy spiteful malefactions, could not o'erbear me,
Think thee not this false, retarded boon
Will soothe my wrath and bend my constant will.
Well, Zeus, thy doubtful mercy comes too late.

ZEUS

Thy haughty obstinacy thou dost love
Far more than thou didst ever cherish justice!
I hoped that thou hadst found thy former wisdom,
That thou wouldst be compliant to my will;
But all in vain has been thy agony.

PROMETHEUS

Why my agony sore troubleth thee
I think I know. When long agone thou didst
Me fix to this sharp rock that thrusts aside
The neighbour clouds, thou thoughtest in thy mind
T'exhibit me to all the universe:
To teach all powers the vain futility
Of flouting thee. That I should stoutly bear
Thy blows and defy thee still, thou thoughtest not;
For still am I the mote that galls thine eye.

But for my unvanquish'd will, thou hadst
Subdued the universe. Thou canst not make me
Feel remorse for that I justly did.
Go work thy will on timid gods and men!
Thou canst not conquer me.

ZEUS

Thou dost too much presume on my forbearance!
Thou wouldst for justice' sake my grace forswear.
Once more vindictive pride comes garb'd in robes
Of righteousness! I tell thee pride, not justice,
Is the ground of thy rude contumely.
Prometheus, thou wast ever proud and wilful;
But now thy judgement hath clean forsaken thee.
What! presumest thou to judge thy lord,
At whose commandment all the world doth tremble?
Knowest thou not that what I will is just,
And justice is whate'er I will? Ages
More shall pass ere I return to thee.

PROMETHEUS

Thy words do well befit the tyrant's tongue.
The universe go shake with thy loud thunder!
I fear it not. It doth only offend my ears.
I would that thou wouldst speed thee on thy way.

ZEUS

                Thus am I requited:
To be so rated by a recreant god!
I pitied thee, and thou didst not a tincture
Of my pity merit. I proffer'd thee
My absolution, if thou wouldst but repent thee
Of thy sin, and thou didst cast it back
Into my face. So be it then, for thou
Shalt have thy will and I will hasten from thee.
But thou, Prometheus, wilt long abide.
Hereafter thou shalt think upon thy folly,
And great disquiet it shall cause thee.

[*Exit* ZEUS. *A peal of thunder. A pause, and then*
PROMETHEUS *speaks.*]

PROMETHEUS

Notwithstanding Zeus' far-reaching wrath,
Mankind I judge deserving of my love.
That I on them bestow'd the boon of fire,
I cannot repent, truly. For that I lovèd
Man and justice best, suffer I must.
But mongst the myriad days that formless lie
Within the vast and teeming womb of time,
I mark that day when Zeus will feel the sting
Of love and ruth, the twin-headed dart,
Sharp pierce his iron breast, wherefor he shall
Let fall his hoarded tears. My torment shall cease,
And we at last shall reconcilèd be.
Grave visaged Justice, she that never sleeps
Nor winks an eye, shall stand upon his right;
Gentle Mercy, with tongue in honey steep'd,
That oft doth close the curtains of her eyes,
Shall kneel upon his left. All this, I say,
Shall come to pass when Cronides a mortal
Will have loved, a maid of wondrous beauty,
Beloved daughter to an Argive king.
By her shall he conceive a son—a son
That he will love as he doth love himself.
As in some fertile vale a tender sapling,
Deep-rooted, grows into a lordly pine,
Far o'ertopping all the other trees
That toward the clouds upthrust their lofty limbs,
So shall this child to manhood grow, surpassing
All the race of humankind: a youth
In beauty like Apollo, like vast Atlas
In his strength. And he, Zeus' noble son,
To me shall come, by deep compassion moved,
To slay the monstrous eagle, glutted with gore,
And burst my bonds asunder. His sinewy hands
Zeus will not stay. Spurning jealous pride,

He will but smile upon his son and weep
For me. Though mortal born, he will not die;
But one day thou, great Zeus, wilt him upraise
Into the heavens with thee to dwell. Through him,
Thy son, shall man's estate exalted be,
And my agony shall not have been in vain.
A fragrant wind of praise will rise from earth,
The gods their envious pride will put aside
And come to thee in peace and perfect concord,
And thou wilt justly rule the universe.
But until Time my prophecy fulfill,
Do what thou wilt, I do defy thee still.

[Curtain drop]

Shorter Poems

Not these new fangled toys, and trimming slight
Which takes our late fantasticks with delight.

— Milton

Autumn Voices

The sun is down, and still the old men sit
Along their narrow bench and talk together.
All else is silent in the autumn dusk;
But they, like locusts on a naked bough,
Talk on and on—of summer-time they talk,
Till darkness comes to lie upon the hills.
And one by one the feeble voices cease.

Fairest Cheek

Suggested by a song
from *The Devil's Law-case* (V. iv)
by John Webster

Fairest cheek and brightest eye
Like subtle perfume fade and die.
Time soon withers all that's fair;
Darkness inundates the air.
Helen adieu, adieu delights
And all bewitching appetites.

For joys that once have been I sigh;
For those that ne'er can be I cry.
Fairest cheek and brightest eye
Like subtle perfume fade and die—
And so must I
And sweet delights
And all bewitching appetites.

Go By, Hieronimo

What thing that lives within the starry compass
Of the universe so keenly feels
The pangs of grief as man? Weeping he comes
Into the world, and at the end he turns
A desolate face unto th'indifferent earth;
And in the interim is he beset
With sorrow, pain, and blasted hopes. In fine,
What is his life but a brief and bitter prelude
To oblivion? Of all the race
There is none happier than he that's born
In silence—with not a single breath to cry,
Nor any tear to shed.
Yet, being thrust into the world, what then?
Why then, methinks, the next in happiness
Is he that can forget himself in madness.
Hang all sages and philosophers!
Madness is a stouter shield by far
Than ever reason was.

The Death of Patroclus

Proud Patroclus at Hector aimed his spear
And hurled it hard; nor did the far-flung missle
Lose its mark, but valiant Hector stooped
And straightway thrust his buckler high to meet it,
The which did rip the buckler from his arm,
And from his head, with ear-offending clang,
Did strike the gleaming helm. Clutching his spear,
Half-stunned, Hector turned and at his foe
He hurled it swiftly. Through Patroclus' shield
And onward through his massy cuirass bore
The wingèd cypress. Through the yielding flesh
It bit, bursting bone and gristle; nor did
It cease its baneful flight, till the brazen head
Cut through the warrior's back and gleamed i' the sun.
Poised upon the brink of life, Patroclus
Grasped with both his hands the gory shaft.
Stone-like he stood, his head in anguish bowed;
Nor did he utter word nor made he moan.
Soon 'gan his broached and shattered frame to sway;
Then fell he softly in a crumpled heap.
And the bright blood spouted forth, drenching
                                        the ground,
And death did shroud him in eternal night.

Hector Slain

What warrior lies here whose arms reflect
The falling sun in tones of awful red!
Are these the arms of Hector, Ilium's shield?
Proud Hector, art thou slain?—thou that bore
The shocks of fifty battles? Then Ilium fall!
Farewell, brave youth. Whilst thou didst stand
                                    and breathe,
No princely foe with cool impunity
Dared touch thy sleeve. Now liest thou in the dust,
Unmindful of the little flies that creep
Upon thy lips.
O royal Zeus, who speakest with the voice
Of wide-resounding thunder; who with thy right hand
The sable sky didst streak with blazing comets;
Whose kingdom is the boundless universe:
Sow fire and pestilence upon the plain
Of Argos! Argive walls encompass round
With noise of war and stench of slaughter'd men,
And let a Grecian Hector fall and bleed
Before a Grecian Troy.

Incident from Homer

When Zeus with Hera lay on misty Ida,
Poseidon shook the walls of Ilium
And Pallas swept the Trojans from the plain.

The Farmer and the Cranes

(Aesop's Fable reversified from a
translation by Donald B. Hull)

A flock of cranes alighted in a field
Of corn. To make them fly away and yield
His land, the farmer twirled an empty sling,
But one that seemed to them a dreadful thing.
And as they watched the angry farmer throw
At them the vacant air, they came to know
That they had naught to fear and need not fly
When threatened thus. The farmer on the sly
Then picked up stones, and with his sling he
                                    flung them—
And all th'astonished cranes screamed when he
                                    stung them.
"Alas, the man will murder us!" they cried.
"Let's fly to Hindustan and there abide.
This man is not content to threat and scare;
He acts in earnest now! My friends, beware!"

Leander to Hero

(Excerpt from an abandoned poem)

Now bright robed Cynthia, gliding 'mongst the stars,
Illumines all the limpid night with beams
Of silver sheen. Lo, how the leafy boughs
Do softly sway in the arms of the wanton wind.
Ah, love, how fresh and delicate this world
Doth seem when thou art near! But let us hence.
I'll be thy knight and thou wilt be my steed.
Come, delightful mare, and let me mount thee,
And let us race across the moonlit meadow.
How closely I shall cling to thee when thou
Wilt lightly leap into the air to prance
Upon the moonbeams! Yet will I spur thee on.
Oh, let us leave this lovely earth awhile
And upward soar among the burning stars.

Science

(A recasting of Shelley's "Ozymandias")

A goddess from supernal regions came
Upon a lifeless orb that once was known
As Earth. And this is all the immortal dame
Beheld: Two vast and trunkless legs of stone
In a desert standing, and near the fallen frame,
Half-sunk, there lay a shattered visage, dread,
With lowering brow and stare unpitying.
These words upon the pedestal she read
(Half scoured they were by some infernal flame):
"My name is *Science* and all men call me *King*.
Look on my works, ye mighty, and despair!"
Nothing beside remains. Round the decay
Of that colossal wreck, boundless and bare
The lone and level sands stretch far away.

PART II

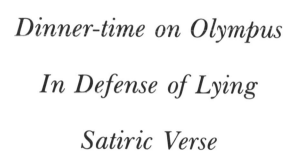

Dinner-time on Olympus

In Defense of Lying

Satiric Verse

Dinner-time on Olympus

A Sacred Farce in One Act

PERSONS OF THE DRAMA

HERA

ZEUS

HERMES

Dinner-time on Olympus

A Sacred Farce in One Act

[*Scene: Olympus. Carbon dioxide clouds, a light covering of snow, and several free-standing Doric columns. Enter* HERA, *followed by* ZEUS, *followed by thunder. Clouds gradually disperse as the scene is played.*]

HERA. Why are you frowning, Zeus? Don't you feel well—or have you mislaid your aegis again?

ZEUS. I feel well enough, I suppose. It is only the weather. Must do something about the weather on this mountain. Just look at those god-damned clouds!

HERA. I wish you wouldn't curse. It sounds so vulgar.

ZEUS. What nonsense. It is only vulgar to curse in vain. Besides, a god may curse anything he pleases.

HERA. You don't look well.

ZEUS. Now that you mention it, Hera, I don't feel perfectly well after all.

HERA. I thought so. That is why the weather is bad. I believe a good dinner would improve your disposition, and the weather too.

ZEUS. Nothing at all the matter with my disposition. You seem to think eating is the answer to any problem.

HERA. It very often is. Even gods need to take some nourishment from time to time. Why are you holding your head?

ZEUS. I think I'm getting a headache.

HERA. Good heavens, I hope it's not another pregnancy! I will not have another Athena in my palace!
[*Aside*] I can bear his vanity, I can even abide his infidelities, but it galls me to the quick to think that any god might reproduce his kind without female assistance. It sets a dangerous precedent and compromises the majesty of our sex. I will not suffer another such indignity again.

ZEUS. This is not a matter for Hephaestus. It is quite an ordinary headache. Well, what are we having for dinner?

HERA. Ambrosia and nectar.

ZEUS. That's all we ever have. Don't you know that I am sick to death of ambrosia and nectar? Can't we ever dine on anything else?

HERA. We are having ambrosia and nectar because ambrosia and nectar are good for us. Aesculapius says that they preserve our immortality and put iron in our ichor.

ZEUS. Aesculapius is nothing but a damnable quack!

HERA. You know very well ambrosia can be enjoyed in a variety of ways. I thought you particularly liked the *mousseline d'ambrosie* Ganymede served you last Thursday.

ZEUS. Ambrosia is ambrosia, and there's an end! Time we tried something else for a change.

HERA. Something else? What else could we possibly have?

ZEUS. Lots of other things we might try. Steak, for instance. Yes, steak and potatoes and perhaps even a good cup of coffee—and afterwards a spot of ouzo, eh?

HERA.   What, dine on steak, potatoes, and coffee? Drink ouzo too? We couldn't do that. What extraordinary ideas you have!

ZEUS.   And why couldn't we? Just answer me that. What is the good of being gods if we can't do as we like?

HERA.   It would look bad. What would all the other gods say? It would set a bad example. You know very well that steak and potatoes and things like that have never been fashionable on Olympus. They are, I believe, consumed only by mortals and their dogs. Consequently, one can hardly suppose that common comestibles like those can be suitable for the tables of divine society!

ZEUS.   That is all very well, but I don't care an obol for fashion. And hang divine society! I tell you, the father of the gods is not one to be ruled by fashion.

HERA.   Ah, there you are mistaken, my dear. Fashion is nothing less than propriety and decorum—at least I am sure that it is so on Olympus—and that is why even Zeus must observe fashion among the gods.

ZEUS.   Well, I doubt that a change in our dinner menu would seriously disturb the universal order.

HERA.   Perhaps not, but it just might give you a bad case of indigestion. Furthermore, no matter how cleverly it is prepared, the food of mortals has the unfortunate property of producing a residuum that is peculiarly offensive to divine sensibilities.

ZEUS.   By Jove, that is a matter I had quite overlooked. But, now I think of it, that is no objection. Nothing offensive can issue from me, for always I am Zeus. An odor of sanctity hangs about me. At any rate, I am quite determined to change my diet.

HERA.   If you are so displeased with our usual fare,

excellent though it is, you might at least consider
sending for something else, something from another
race of gods—those three who inhabit the other side
of the heavens, for instance.

ZEUS.　Who? Oh, you mean those Jewish fellows?

HERA.　Jewish? I thought they were Christian gods.

ZEUS.　Pretty much the same thing, isn't it? In their
mortal worshipers, at least, I can perceive very little
difference, if any at all.

HERA.　One distinction is that Jews believe in one god,
Christians in three.

ZEUS.　Yet Christians profess the same curious
monotheism as Jews in a way, don't they?

HERA.　Perhaps. If that is the case, however, it certainly
appears to me that neither Christians nor Jews can
be very religious. To deny all gods but one, or even
three, is not only ungracious—it is almost atheistic!
Besides, Christian theology seems unnecessarily
complex and mysterious. Let me see, is it three gods
in one person or three persons in one god? Three
gods riding in one chariot or one god riding in
three chariots?

ZEUS.　There are really three of them as I recall, and
they share the same office in partnership—a
triumvirate of sorts. Nothing mysterious about it.
You know very well how mortal worshipers can
complicate things and botch them up in their own
little minds. Look how they misrepresented us in the
old days. But I still think at least one of those chaps
is Jewish—the oldest one. He looks Jewish.

HERA.　I have heard that he looks like you.

ZEUS.　Oh, that has been a common misconception ever
since I consented to sit for Michelangelo in the
Sistine Chapel. Now why are you smiling?

HERA.　To think how furious Julius II would have been
had he known.

ZEUS.　Whose idea do you think it was?

HERA.　Good heavens, do you mean to say the pope
wanted you to sit for Jehovah's portrait? How
extraordinary!

ZEUS.　Not extraordinary at all. You forget that the
pope was Italian, and Italians, as everyone knows,
are pagans at heart. If they were not, they could not
possibly have invented the Renaissance.

HERA.　Yes, that's very true, and it was the Renaissance
that gave us a new lease on immortality.

ZEUS.　Well, I'm afraid our lease is almost up, my dear.
See how these mortals forget the legacy of their
ancient past—both beauty, reason, and the arts—and
run pell-mell into another age of night.

HERA.　And after that, in Time's dilatory course,
another Renaissance.

ZEUS.　Possibly, possibly. But in the meantime back to
more serious matters. Those foreign gods dine on
something called *manna*, and I understand that it is
quite delicious.

HERA.　Do you suppose we could make a trade?

ZEUS.　Don't know, really, but certainly worth a try,
what? I'll send Hermes. He knows his way round. If
anyone can find a way, he will. I feel better already.

[*Clouds clear, sunshine breaks through.*]

HERA.　Hermes is quite the most subtle and cunning of
the gods.

ZEUS.　Yes, that is why he is the god of physicians and
thieves.

HERA.　Even Hermes will not have an easy time of it.
Those foreign gods are an unsociable lot, you know.
They always act as if they hardly know us.

ZEUS.   Yes, I know. Their mortal devotees have pulled down our statues and destroyed our temples. Don't believe in us, too. What fanatics they are. Why, they have even burned down the libraries of our worshipers.

HERA.   Yes, zealotry has done its worst. What between the incendiary reforms of Christians and the righteous depredations of Moslems, it is remarkable that any trace of civilization has survived. Of course those barbarities occurred a long time ago, though it seems like yesterday. We have no worshipers left on earth now—except for a few at Oxford.

ZEUS.   And not a bad thing. All those mortals ever did was beg us for favors and blame us any time things went wrong for them. Good riddance, I say. Let those three Christian chaps have all the trouble now. Serves them right, you know. I understand, however, that the mother of the second one—the Son I think he's called—is a decent sort. She seems, at least, more genial than the others and is even known to smile at times. Hermes says one might almost mistake her for a Pagan. Pity she's not a goddess.

HERA.   Yes, I met her once. Such a nice woman, too— but not very bright. Two thousand years old and still a virgin!

ZEUS.   Not so loud, my dear. Hercules might hear you, and you know how he is about virgins.[1] Certainly don't want any trouble from that chaste quarter of heaven. Perhaps it may be expedient to deal through that admirable lady, but it would hardly seem appropriate for Zeus to address anyone but the regnant deity of the place, would it? Protocol, you

---

1. In what must surely have been his most heroic labor, Hercules is said to have deflowered fifty virgins in one night. As a consequence, all fifty became mothers. According to a well-known tradition first recorded by Procopius, the ancient Feast of the Multiple Conceptions is thought to be the origin of Mother's Day.

know. We may, of course, avail ourselves of the lady's good offices should the need arise, but I shall certainly direct Hermes to look up the very first person of that holy trinity—that is, if he can manage to get by all those officious angels and saints. The place is positively crawling with them. Hermes!

[*Enter* HERMES.]

HERMES. You called, my lord?

ZEUS. Yes. What kept you? Want you to take a message to a god called Jehovah.

HERMES. Jehovah, my lord?

ZEUS. Yes, Jehovah. You remember him, Hermes—the old fellow who is always saying that he created the universe.

HERMES. Oh, the Semitic chap. Why, the way he talks one would think he was the only god around. I'll do my best, my lord, but it won't be easy. The place is positively crawling with officious angels and saints.

HERA. I hear they are quite struck with their own perfection.

HERMES. Yes. That is precisely why they never cease applauding their creator. At any rate, I shall disguise myself to look like one of them. It is the only way to get through.

ZEUS. And how will you do that?

HERMES. Wear a bright halo, direct my gaze upward toward the empyrean, and look like a man who has endured four or five days of acute constipation.

ZEUS. Good. Hope it works.

HERMES. It always does, my lord.

ZEUS. But you must remember to address him in verse. Gods will not stir for prose.

HERMES. I will, my lord.

[ZEUS *begins writing.*]

HERA. Do you pass yourself off as a Christian or a Jew?

HERMES. Neither, my lady. I almost always say I am a Presbyterian. You see, most of the angels there are Presbyterians.

HERA. How can you tell?

HERMES. They look so unhappy.

HERA. Ah, that is no doubt a natural consequence of their spiritual perfection.

HERMES. Yes, my lady. Of course I could not possibly pass for a Jew. I should be found out immediately.

HERA. Yes, but that might easily be remedied by a tunic or a loincloth, I presume. In any case, circumcision seems to me an entirely unnecessary custom. I cannot see what practical purpose it can possibly serve.

HERMES. Even though it does not benefit the circumcised in any way, it does seem to serve a practical purpose, my lady. Besides being a convenient mark of sectarian identification, circumcision produces a singular by-product, a mindless material out of which Charismatics and Maryknoll Marxists are created.

HERA. Ah, I *knew* there was some reason why I instinctively disliked the practice.

HERMES. Yes, my lady. It is not a very pleasant subject.

HERA. You seem, Hermes, to be extraordinarily well-versed in the rites and customs of these peculiar oriental cults. I suppose that you know something about a book they call the Bible. It is a work they appear to set much store by, is it not?

HERMES. It is. I have seen their sacred book and it contains passages of grace and beauty, but there is not a trace of mirth in it. What little humor it contains seems entirely unintentional.

HERA.   But surely there is mirth in their heaven.

HERMES.   None at all, my lady. Everyone there is perfectly serious.

HERA.   Well, it certainly sounds to me like a curious place.

HERMES.   Indeed it is. In that part of heaven no one ever laughs.

HERA.   How sad.

HERMES.   That, in fact, is why there are no literary critics there.

HERA.   That is strange. I should have thought that literary critics were excluded for their arrogance and abominable taste.

HERMES.   Not at all, my lady. These are considered but slight faults in them. In their case allowances are made; for critics, after all, are merely harmless creatures to whom no sensible man pays the least regard. Their one serious fault is that they sometimes laugh. You see, whenever critics encounter each other, they cannot keep from laughing.

HERA.   Well, that is quite understandable. Charlatans will recognize their kind. But why laughter should be forbidden at all, I cannot imagine.

[*Having finished writing, Zeus hands the message to Hermes.*]

ZEUS.   Here is the message, Hermes. Pray read it first, and then I shall seal it.

[Hermes *reads silently.*]

HERMES.   Is that all, my lord?

ZEUS.   Yes. Sick to death of nectar and ambrosia. Incidentally, Hermes, have you ever tasted *manna?*

HERMES.   I have tasted it several times. Very good, too—especially with peanut butter.

HERA.   Peanut butter? I do not know what peanut butter is, but I am sure that I abhor it. It sounds obscene.

ZEUS.   Where in heaven's name did you find peanut butter?

HERMES.   Southern Baptist saints use it all the time. Of course, those from Texas invariably prefer ketchup, but ketchup is rarely found in heaven. Indeed, now that I think of it, Texans are rarely found there.

HERA.   Ah, in that case heaven cannot be quite so bad as it is cracked up to be—in spite of all those lugubrious angels. One can always put up with Presbyterians. Texans are quite another matter.

ZEUS.   Thank you, Hermes. That will be all. Now take along two baskets of ambrosia and a cask of nectar, my second best vintage, and return with all the manna you can carry. Be sure it's top grade. But you haven't yet told me what manna tastes like.

HERMES.   Do you really want to know?

ZEUS.   Indeed, by all means.

HERMES.   Like lobster thermidor and a fine vintage *Chateau Olivier* to a Frenchman, roast beef and ale to an Englishman, and hamburger and Coca-Cola to an American.

HERA.   Well, fortunately we are not American.

ZEUS.   This manna is truly remarkable. Can hardly wait to try some. But tell me, Hermes, how does it taste to an Olympian god?

HERMES.   Why, just like ambrosia and nectar.

[*Low, rumbling thunder. Exit* ZEUS, *frowning, as clouds cover the stage.*]

In Defense of Lying

The Lord is my shepherd; I shall not want.
He maketh me to lie. . . .

—Ps. 23:1–2

Every man of sense knows that lying, the most misunderstood and maligned of all the arts, is indispensable to civilized society; yet hardly anyone has a good word to say about it, at least in public, so ingrained has been the common prejudice against it. Despite that prejudice, however, it is my intention to uncover lies about truth and to tell the truth about lies. My task is more hazardous than arduous, but to combat ignorance in defense of a just cause is a pleasure well worth the risk.

The truth has been vastly overrated. Telling the truth is neither difficult nor virtuous. It requires no wisdom, no ingenuity, and no imagination; indeed, it is the divine gift of imagination that enables man (and maketh me) to lie. Any fool can tell the truth. Fools generally do. Rarely does a fool tell a lie. When he does, it is usually unintentional. He blunders into it. Even when he lies intentionally, he is almost always unconvincing; and that is due not only to his want of art, but to his insincerity. One must be sincere about one's lying if one is to be taken seriously. Sincere liars command our admiration; insincere liars deserve our scorn, for they are nothing more than impostors. They give liars a bad name.

There is something indecent about the naked truth; it should never be put on public display unless it is appropriately dressed. Certainly one cannot always tell the truth

133

and be courteous too. Show a man his faults and he will hate you for it; call them virtues and he will be your friend. "In vino veritas," the proverb says, which means, "Truthful men are like drunkards, for they are blunt and rude."[1] A gentleman, however, is a man who has learned when to lie. That may be his chief accomplishment.

The language of love and diplomacy is compounded of lies; without them polite society would be quite impossible. To his son (Sherlock), Oliver Wendell Holmes wrote, "A man who will not lie to a woman has very little consideration for her feelings." A bastion of society is marriage, and there is no greater foe to marriage than truth, no greater defender than lies. Nevertheless, neither lover, nor spouse, nor diplomat should ever openly admit he lies; and yet, even so prudent a man as Sir Henry Wotton once fell into that deplorable error. In what could only have been a rare moment of distraction, the celebrated diplomat wrote in the visitors' book of his host in Augsburg the following remark: "An ambassador is an honest man sent abroad to lie for the sake of his country."[2] For that apposite but undiplomatic observation—for telling the truth about lying—Wotton incurred the displeasure of James I and thereby came close to ending his distinguished career.

Just as lies are not always salutary, so the truth is not always reprehensible; yet I have known two or three grave and honest men who will habitually confuse truth with virtue, never realizing they are not the same: truth is not always beneficial, though virtue is. Loving truth for its own sake makes no more sense, I think, than loving fire for its own sake: the value of truth depends upon the use to which it is put. Some truths are good, some bad, and some

---

1. My loose translation.
2. The more familiar translation from Wotton's Latin reads "sent to lie abroad," a syntactical arrangement that creates a pun not present (and not possible) in the original, which reads, *Legatus est vir bonus, peregre missus ad mentiendum Reipub. [sic] causa.* (See L. P. Smith, *The Life and Letters of Sir Henry Wotton* (Oxford: Clarendon Press, 1907), Vol. I, p. 49.

indifferent. Sometimes the truth is merely the sort of thing a man says when he can't think of anything else to say. At best the truth is simply utilitarian in function and pedestrian in character: its proper use is to help carry on the tedious but necessary business of the world. Its abuse, however, is the very head and source of half the world's afflictions. In the hands of unreasoning zealots, the truth is always hazardous and often lethal. One may draw from history innumerable instances of outrages committed in the name of truth, but there is no need to weary the reader by recounting instances that would only corroborate what he already knows.

Plato declared in *The Republic* that all poets are liars and that Homer is, consequently, the foremost of liars. Who would question the accuracy of Plato's observation? One can only imagine how dull and banal the *Iliad* would have been had Homer confined himself to the truth. Instead, to the greater glory of literature, the poet elevated his tale with magnificent lies, framing the heroic dimensions of Hector and Achilles and amplifying the beauty of Helen. There are no better liars than poets and no better poets than liars. Consider John Keats, who said, "Beauty is truth, truth beauty." Now that, of course, is a deliberate lie; but it is beautiful, and that makes all the difference. It is a poetic fiction and therefore transcends mere truth. To apply prosaic tests of logic to a poetic fiction is absurd. Who would propose to break a butterfly upon a wheel?

The art of poetry, as Horace said, does not admit of mediocrity. Neither does the art of lying. Just as only the best verse merits the name of poetry, so only the best prevarications deserve to be called lies. It is not enough to be merely a competent liar as it is to be, say, a competent lawyer or brigand, physician or thief. In lying, as in poetry, one must either excel or fail. There is no middle ground. Unless he is amusing, like the politician, whom no one takes seriously, the imperfect liar is doomed to failure: he is worse off than one who cannot lie at all. Christopher Marlowe called poetry (which is as much to say, lying) "the highest reaches of the human wit." Lying at its best demands brilliance of conception, intrepidity of execution, and—above all—an unfailing memory.

It is often assumed that modern literary critics are liars, pretending to more knowledge than they possess and to aesthetics so sublime and profound that they consider the vast resources of the English language too meager to sustain the weight of their thought. Thus, striving to surmount the dialectical inadequacies of English (as they imagine) and thereby shunning its simple clarity, they concoct new tongues which gain in obscurity what they lose in beauty. Though no mean critic himself, Hazlitt concludes his essay "On the Ignorance of the Learned" with these words:

> If we wish to know the force of human genius we should read Shakespeare. If we wish to see the insignificance of human learning we may study his commentators.

The innocent reader approaches the critic in hope of finding an interpreter, one who will illuminate a text and act as a catalyst between the author and the reader. If critics ever served such useful functions, they have long since abandoned them in favor of more metaphysical pursuits. Why must they labor to extract meaning *ex littera* when they can create it *ex nihil?* No catalysts are they, but, confusion worse confounded, they make the recondite abstruse and common sense difficult. Like the obscurantist authors they delight in, these critics would have us think they mean more than they say when they say more than they mean. I do not know that they are truthful, but I doubt that they are mendacious. Lying is, after all, a rational art, and modern literary critics have nothing to do with reason. That is why they are best understood by those who have lost their power of reasoning (other critics, mostly). No one else can or ever could make much of what they say—not since the lamentable death of the last Sibyl, at any rate.

Not all liars are entirely admirable, but good lying can mitigate many a serious fault. There are, for example, the politicians, a race of indefatigable mischief-makers whose job it is to annoy their fellow men by continually enacting foolish laws. Yet, it must be allowed that their vices are in some measure extenuated by their ingenious lies. Politicians are not the world's most convincing prevaricators, but even though they are not to be found in the first rank of the art, they are immensely entertaining. Unfortunately, from time to time society is moved by a morbid compulsion to reform the politicians. Whenever such an occasion arises, politicians are invariably called upon to renounce lying. That is a mistake. Lying is, after all, their only redeeming virtue. Without it, politicians would be quite insufferable.

Today's social reformers, a species of moralists variously known as sociologists, anthropologists, and liberal judges, are admirable liars. No other social reformers are so ostentatiously moral as liberal judges, and few liars are as serenely confident. Profoundly conscious of the benefactions they have liberally bestowed upon mankind, they wear their robes with such a show of gravity that all may see how they are God's anointed. Filled as they are with spiritual pride, they cannot choose but to lie with confidence. Hence, sooner or later, they come to believe the juridical myths of their own invention. Whether they are busy reconstructing society or humanizing criminal justice, liberal judges are almost always animated by a certain the-Lord-God-made-them-all kind of reasoning. So relentless are they in their pursuit of enlightened justice, they are not unwilling to hazard the sacrifice of a half-dozen or more innocent lives, if necessary, in order to reform one unfortunate criminal. Their sense of justice, like the grace of God, passeth all understanding.

Sociologists and anthropologists, like the liberal judges and other philanthropists who draw upon their wisdom, frequently lie on the principle, "This should be true, ergo this *is* true." It is the kind of reasoning which, in earlier times, produced the now venerable fiction, "All men are created equal." Most truths said to be "self-evident" are really venerable fictions—benevolent lies so often repeated that they cease to be questioned and, when uttered by an idealist as eloquent as Thomas Jefferson, so flawlessly phrased that they become a kind of romantic poetry, exempt from the prosaic demands of common sense. A statesman may be eloquent, but no one has ever accused a sociologist or an anthropologist of phrasing anything flawlessly. Apart from a want of eloquence, the only thing which makes the social reformer inferior to the poet in his practice of the art is that the social reformer never finds it easy to distinguish the difference between veracity and mendacity, but a good poet always knows when he is lying. The best art is deliberate.

As liars poets are rivalled only by historians and theologians. It seems remarkable that those who are loudest in their denunciation of lying are usually among the art's most adept practitioners. The chief purpose of history is to record the lies of mankind for the edification of posterity. The truth is known to make men miserable. Through the artful fabrications of historians, however, men of all nations and creeds may preserve entire their sense of superiority and self-esteem; for there are enough versions of history to satisfy all tastes. One may survey the past through spectacles of any color: Marxist-red, capitalist-green, nationalist-true-blue, journalist-yellow, feminist-pink, or moralist-opaque. All men believe what they wish to believe, and that accounts for the extraordinary popularity of history and religion. Indeed, history and religion supply us with some of our most gratifying prejudices.

Man cherishes his prejudices. Acknowledging them is quite another matter (we call them by other names). In spite of all reason, we are quick to embrace facts which flatter our prejudices and ignore facts which cast doubts upon them. We need never be troubled by truths that do

Jonah, about to be the author of the greatest fish story ever told.

not contribute to our happiness as long as we can conveniently dismiss them out-of-hand or else rationalize them into oblivion.

The curious expression one often sees on the faces of saints in Baroque paintings and sculptures was caused neither by spiritual ecstasy nor by acute constipation. A look like that could arise only from the constant strain of trying to tell the truth. Fortunately, few Christians in these more enlightened times pay the smallest attention to outworn precepts against lying, at least as far as their own behavior is concerned. Christianity has a wonderful capacity for progressing with the times, for Christianity and common sense are not necessarily incompatible. Besides, the change is not without scriptural precedence.

Does not the Bible itself proclaim the divine origin of lies? Witness the fabulous tales of Moses parting the Red Sea, Noah and the ark, Jonah and the whale, the walrus and the carpenter, and many more besides. Read *Genesis* (5:17), where God in His infinite wisdom enjoins Adam, our father, not to seek the truth:

> But of the tree of knowledge of good and evil
> thou shalt not eat of it; for in the day that thou
> eatest thereof thou shalt surely die.

Obviously, one who seeks the truth must of necessity seek knowledge, and that knowledge must not be circumscribed, for it must be knowledge of both good and evil. Is it not therefore manifest that man's fall was occasioned by his own depraved lust for truth, the forbidden fruit whose mortal taste brought death into the world?[3]

---

3. In a recent number of *The Micanopy Literary Supplement*, a critic (John Buckingham) erroneously accused me of plagiarizing from John Milton's *Paradise Lost* the concluding relative clause of this paragraph. What we have here is a coincidental similarity of phrasing. If any reader should turn to *Paradise Lost* (I. 2–3), he will find that the lines I have been accused of stealing are still there, intact. So much for Buckingham.

II

"Who killed Cock Robin?"
"I did," said the sparrow,
"With my little bow and arrow."
"No, I did," said the wren,
"With my little pen."

The truth can be dangerous in the hands of a wise man; in the hands of a journalist it can spark disaster. Adam sought the truth regardless of the consequences; in these days journalists seek to publish the truth regardless of the consequences, and the toll in reputations blasted, governments demolished, and societies convulsed is staggering. They make a wasteland and call it *news.* Yet, as God is my witness, I would not have the reader think that I concur with the opinions of their more venomous detractors, who regard them as no better than jackals, assassins, and boils

What, Cock Robin dead? Oh, treacherous avicide!

upon the buttocks of the body politic. As a dispassionate observer, I scorn intemperate reflections of that nature— no matter how apt they may be. It would please me much to say a few kind words in their defense, but only a first-rate liar could do them justice.

It should be kept in mind that journalists are seldom content simply to take the truth as they find it, for that is no longer the fashion. So devoted to the truth are they that, by hook or crook, they must improve upon it. For them the bare truth is too prosaic. Hence, according to the golden rule of expedience, they can modify it subtly or amplify it prodigiously.

In his recent address to the *New Jersey Chapter of the Society for the Prevention of Uncharitable Exposure in the Press*, his Excellency the Archbishop of Cranbury applied these memorable words of George Chapman (ca. 1603) to modern journalism:

> She feeds on outcast entrails like a kite;
> In which foul heap, if any ill lies hid,
> She sticks her beak into it, shakes it up,
> And hurls it all abroad, that all may view it.
> Corruption is her nutriment; but touch her
> With any precious ointment, and you kill her:
> Where she finds any filth in men, she feasts,
> And with her black throat bruits it through
>   the world
> Being sound and healthful; but if she but taste
> The slenderest pittance of commended virtue,
> She surfeits of it, and is like a fly
> That passes all the body's soundest parts,
> And dwells upon the sores; or if her squint eye
> Have power to find none there, she forges some:
> She makes that crooked ever which is straight.
>
> *Bussy D'Ambois* (II.i)

Whatever truth may lie in the charge, I think, with all due respect, that this prince of the Church might have displayed greater charity. It is only with reluctance that I cite him—more to show by way of contrast the moderation of my own criticism than to imply the justice of his.

Not everyone reputed to be a liar can lay just claim to that appellation, and it is sometimes hard to distinguish an authentic liar from a charlatan. To call journalists liars would be (to adopt a Churchillian phrase) a *terminological inexactitude.* Journalists are masters of deception, but they are not true liars since there is nothing at all creative in what they do. They are merely common news-mongers who have acquired a certain skill in sensationalizing the truth and misrepresenting it. Journalists fall short because they lack the imagination, the intelligence, and the good taste of authentic liars.

God knows, the plain truth is bad enough. As Abraham Lincoln said, "Let the truth be known and we are soon found out." (I quote from memory.) That is why we fear the truthful man and love the liar. Truth has destroyed more reputations than lies have, and damaged reputations are not soon mended. It takes a lie a long time to overtake the truth.

It is madness for man to worship the truth. The truth is often cruel and inexorable. That is usually why the truth hurts. Without the ameliorating influence of lies, we should all recognize ourselves and each other for what we really are. Few of us could manage to face a revelation so bleak and demoralizing. Years of salutary lying have purchased for us the good opinion of those we love. It would be heartless to undeceive them. In a larger sense, without the benison of lies our world would soon be shorn of half its poetry and charm. Man needs his illusions. They are a great conserver of his sanity. Without them we would lose our self-esteem, our hopes, our dreams, and life itself would soon become a desert, barren and untenable.

Satiric Verse

Now, grim Reproof, swell in my rough-hewed rhyme,
That thou may'st vex the guilty of our time.

—John Marston

A Purge for Lovers
or
A Fig for Priapus!

Satire III from *The Scourge of Vacuity*

Difficilis est satiram non scribere.[1]

—Juvenal

I cannot help but play the satirist
When I behold a love-sick amorist
Who swears he dies for love and naught can quench
The flames that burn him save his pretty wench.
I cannot bear to hear him eulogize
His "peerless love" and then anatomize
"The fairest Eden that was ever seen,"
Her beauties cap-à-pie and all between,
And wish he were her bodice or perhaps
Her brooch, that he might lie between her paps.
I know where his imagination lies—
'Tis not so near her heart as to her thighs.

That bestial fornication men are quick
To gloss with scented flowers of rhetoric,
For all its masks and fair disguises wrought
By poets, lovers, and other fools is naught
But nature's way to ease a costive state
Of genitalia and perpetuate
Upon this dunghill of the universe
A race of fools. How many reams of verse
And clouds of breath have been disgorged to hail
The lewd convulsions of a vile entrail!

---

1. "It is difficult not to write satire."

A Perfect Intellectual

Satire V from *The Scourge of Vacuity*

Stultum facit fortuna quem vult perdere.[1]

—Publilius Syrus

The Liberal I sing, thrice blessed sage—
Presiding spirit of this tawdry age.
No prejudice has he, but, Argus-eyed,
He sees of every question every side.
At Berkeley he was trained to keep his mind
Wide open—at both ends. He's not the kind
To hasten to a rash decision; no,
Enlightened men act seldom and think slow.
Asked once if he'd have lemon with his tea,
He thought the problem over carefully:
For thirty days he thought, in deep seclusion,
Until he found a tentative conclusion.

While Jack Straw and his envious rout rebel,
Making an ordered land disordered hell,
He sits and listens to a cleric bray
The Gospel of St. Marx the livelong day.
"Social justice" is a text and theme
Progressive parsons hold in high esteem.
With such a passion did this cleric speak,
He broke his wind and scarlet flushed his cheek;

---

1. "Whom Fortune would destroy she renders foolish."

But though he preached right on, with unctuous art,
I swear there was more matter in the f—t.
The Liberal thought them both extraordinary
And praised the text and cheered the commentary.
In all things social and political
He is a perfect intellectual.
So far backward leans he, I'll be bound,
He scrapes his head behind him on the ground;
And thus, for fairness' sake, his head is bald.
His knees, I understand, are somewhat galled,
For on the starry sky he stares and stares
And stumbles into ditches unawares.

As he was sailing southward last November
With his mother and some UN member
(A delegate from Gambia, I think),
A tidal wave o'erwhelmed them in a wink.
Alas, his guest and mother could not swim,
And each in turn for help cried out to him.
When dire necessity demands decision,
Then does he act with rare dispatch and vision:
He sadly left his mother to her fate
And saved the drowning UN delegate.
It was a selfless and unprejudiced deed.
The priceless Freedom Medal was his meed.

Retraction

With grievous shame and sorrow I append
These postscript lines to tell the tragic end
Of him I mocked in rude, satiric jest.
When sorrow bids us speak, grave words are best;
And therefore I discard my cynic guise
To prove the man I wronged was truly wise.
Not long ago—about a week or two—
While following a bluebird as it flew

Into a wood, this liberal-minded man
Soon lost his way. Undaunted, he began
To seek the proper path, but then a fog
Obscured his sight. He walked into a bog,
And though the water crept up to his nose,
Yet forward strode he as the water rose.
Reactionary fools might turn around
And then retrace their steps to higher ground;
But this enlightened liberal pushed on,
And soon all mortal trace of him was gone.
Alas, what can I say? The man is dead.
But his creed lives on: "A liberal moves ahead."

A Fool That Flaunts His Paltry Art

Basta! Basta!

A plague upon this fusty courtier!
'Sfoot, he scrapes his untuned instrument,
Bawls tearful ballads, making wretched faces
All the while, and thereby thinks himself
A rare musician. O for a rasping tongue
That I might rail upon the strutting ape,
This don magnifico! It rends my heart
To hear how rudely he assaults the Muse.
I swear he knows but four or five vile tunes,
And these he iterates incessantly,
Each time a little worse than that before,
Roughly battering the captive ears
Of his excruciated auditors.
Lord, with what a haughty pride this fool
Doth flaunt his paltry art—O villainy!—
As if he were Apollo's very jewel.
                              Oh rare!

Counterblast

Well then, I am an ass. But let that go.
Hath not the world grown asinine? Why, tut,
What is't to be an ass when in a world
Of asses we must live! Why, look where sits
My lord high justice, a most judicious ass,
And near the bench a lawyer stands and lies
To free a homicide and fill a purse—
A quibbling ass obstructing truth and reason.
Yon mincing pedagogue can bend and twist
A lad into a form of learned ass.
Who's this stalks by with Bible in his hand
And melancholy eyes turn'd to the ground?
A Puritan—your most religious ass.
Lo, what's he that rides in coach of state?—
Why, 'tis the royal ass that rules the rest.

A Judicious Ass

Timon Says

'Tis good to wake, yet better far to sleep.
To laugh is best, though sometimes we must weep.
'Tis good to speak, but better to be quiet.
'Tis good to dine, but better yet to diet.
'Tis good to journey, better to remain;
And good to think, but better to refrain.
'Tis better to be single than to wed
And not as good to live as to be dead.

A Slender Lad

That I Should Bear It!

My envious enemies, finding the armor
Of my virtues proof against their darts
Of malice, now stoop to turn their desperate aim
Unto my somewhat portly body. I will
Not lie. There are some dainty chairs I dare
Not sit in and perhaps some narrow portals
That impede my progress, but they that call me
Corpulent do grossly lie. Jove,
How petty men do ever love to find
And magnify the slightest imperfections
In the great! That I should bear it! Hah,
I scorn their filthy calumny. Lo,
When I stand thus, sucking in my belly,
Do I not almost pass for a slender lad?

Your Only Democrat

What, call Drunkenness a tyrant? You lie!
Why, Drunkenness is your only democrat:
All men he levels to a common plane,
Changing kings, philosophers, and priests
Unto the likeness of depravèd beasts.

Envoy

Not with rancor do I now indite
These postscript numbers. If my words offend,
Pray blame not me, for in my throat they burn,
And I must cough them up or else I choke.
Once past my lips, they cannot be recalled,
Nor should they be—take them as you will.
When justice bids us speak, plain terms are best.

My patient muse disdains the empty plaudits
Of this gross and gaudy age that is
In nothing constant save inconstancy—
This age when brutish rudeness is exalted,
And savage blackamoors in knightly capes
Infest the council chambers of the great,
And scholars defecate in Phoebus' shrines,
And poets piss into the Pierian spring,
And Merit, humbled to a common plane,
Must live to curse the gothic night in vain.

Glossary to the Plays

Abbreviations:
   conj., conjunction.
   int.adv., interrogative adverb.
   lit., literally.
   p.ppl., present participle.
   pa.ppl., past participle.
   rel.adv., relative adverb.
   sb., substantive.
   v., verb.
   var(s)., variant(s).

Key to the pronunciation:
   āble, ēqual, īce, ōver.
   Every *ch* pronounced *k*.
   every *ae* and *oe* diphthong pronounced *e*.

Ach′.er.on. A river of the underworld.

Ad′.a.mant, sb. A fabulous stone of impenetrable hardness.

Ae′.gis. Attribute of Zeus and Athena, usually represented in the form of a goatskin. When Zeus shakes the aegis, a fearsome thunder-storm ensues.

Aes.cu.lā′.pi.us (Asclepius). Hero and god of healing.

Ae′.son. King of Iolcus and father of Jason (q.v.).

Al.cī′.dēs. "Descendant of Alcaeus," a patronymic denoting Heracles (Hercules), whose stepfather was Amphitryon, son of Alcaeus and King of Argos. Heracles was the son of Zeus by Alcmena, wife of Amphitryon.

Am.brō′.sia. Food of the gods.

An, conj. If.

A.pī′.a. An ancient name for the Peloponessus.

159

Apollō (Phoebus, Hyperion, Helios). Sun god, patron of poetry and other arts, son of Zeus by Leto (Latona) and twin brother of Artemis (q.v.).

Argo. Ship of Jason and the Argonauts.

Argos. A celebrated city of the Peloponessus.

Ar′.te.mis (Diana, Phoebe, Cytherea). Goddess of the moon, patroness of the hunt and of chastity, daughter of Zeus by Leto, and twin sister of Apollo.

Astonied, p.ppl. Astonished; stunned; lit., struck by a thunderbolt.

At′.ro.pos. Most dreaded of the three sister goddesses called the Fates or the Parcae, she cuts the thread of every human life. See *Fates*.

A.ver′.nus. A stagnant, pestiferous lake in Campania (q.v.), regarded as an entrance to the underworld.

Be′.li.dēs. Daughters of Belus who, for plotting the murder of their cousins, were condemned eternally to carry water in broken urns.

Belike, adv. Perhaps; probably.

Betimes, adv. Early; soon.

Blasted, pa.ppl. Blown on balefully; blighted.

Bootless. To no avail; futile.

Bō′.rē.as. God of the north wind; the north wind.

Bourn, sb. Boundary.

Cam.pa′.nia. A region on the western coast of Italy, immediately south of Latium; its principal city was Capua.

Castalia. A fountain sacred to the Muses, situated on the slopes of Mount Parnassus. Its waters inspire those who drink of it.

Cē′.rēs (Demeter). Goddess of grain or vegetation; mother of Proserpina (Persephone).

Cim.mē′.ri.an, adj. Pertaining to Cimmeria, a mythical land of mist and darkness; hence, profoundly dark.

Clept, pa.ppl. Named; called.

Cly′.me.nē. Mother of Prometheus, Epimetheus, Menoetius, and Atlas.

Co.cy′.tus. A river in the underworld.

Col′.chis. An Asian kingdom situated on the Euxine (Black) Sea, where Jason sought and found the Golden Fleece.

Contemn, v. Scorn; hold in contempt.

Con′.tu.ma.cy. Rebellious stubbornness; perverse and obstinate resistance of and disobedience to authority; insolent defiance.

Con′.tume.ly. Scornful rudeness; insolent reproach.

Cor′.us.cā.ting, p.ppl. Emitting vivid flashes of light; sparkling.

Crescent, adj. Ripening; growing; increasing.

Cro′.ni.dēs, sb. Zeus; lit., "son of Cronus," a patronymic. Also, Cronion.

Diana. See *Artemis.*

Dis. The underworld; Erebus.

Dī′.um. A place in southern Pieria where Orpheus, repining after his unhappy quest, renounced the company of women, thereby offending a wild band of feminists (Maenads), who slew him and cast his severed head into the Hebrus River.

Dō.dō′.na. An oracle of Zeus, the most ancient of oracles. Priests interpreted the god's voice from the rustling of leaves in the sacred grove of oaks. The mast of the Argo, endowed with prophetic power, was fashioned from an oak of Dodona.

Doom, sb. Judgment or sentence.

Dryad. A wood nymph.

Enjoined, v. Commanded; directed or imposed by authoritative order.

Er′.e.bus. the underworld. According to some poets, the region between the upper world and the underworld beyond the Styx.

E.rin′.y.ēs. The Furies (q.v.).

Eu.men′.i.dēs. Ironic name (*viz.,* "the gracious ones" or "the kind-hearted ones") for the Furies (q.v.).

Ex′.e.crate, v. Curse; denounce.

Eux′.ine Sea. The Black Sea.

Ex.ig′.u.ous, adj. Meager; scanty in measure; minute.

Ex.sur′.gent, adj. Rising up pre-eminently.

Fates. The Parcae; mighty goddesses who preside over the birth, life, and death of mankind. They are three sisters: Clotho, Lachesis, and Atropos. Clotho, the youngest, presides over the moment of birth, holding in her hand a distaff; Lachesis spins out all the events of human lives; and Atropos, the eldest, severs the thread of life with a pair of scissors.

For that, conj. Because.

Fulgent, adj. Shining brightly; gleaming.

Furies (Furiae). Three sister goddesses of vengeance, or divine justice. Also called Erinyes or Eumenides.

Gall, v. Make sore; chafe.

Glister, v. Glisten.

Gōrgons. Three sister daemons whose hideous aspect turns the beholder to stone. They are Stheno, Euryale, and Medusa.

Grīpe, sb. Grasp; clutch.

Gull, sb. One who is gullible, or easily deceived; a fool.

Hē′.li.os. The sun god, usually identified with Apollo.

Hel′.les.pont. The Dardanelles.

He.phaes′.tus (Vulcan). God of fire and forger of Zeus' thunderbolts; smithy of the gods.

Her′.a.clēs (Hercules). Demigod son of Zeus by Alcmena. See *Alcides.*

Hymen (Hymenaeus). God of marriage.

Ī′.chor. Blood of the gods.

Ī′.o. A Greek exclamation of joy or triumph.

Ix.ī′.on. A king of Thessaly. For his attempted seduction of Hera, Zeus struck him with a thunderbolt and confined him to Tartarus where he is bound to a perpetually moving wheel.

Jā′.son. Leader of the Argonauts. He sailed to Colchis in quest of the Golden Fleece, in which enterprise he thrived through the aid of the Colchian princess and sorcerer, Medea.

La.cō′.ni.a (vars., Lacedaemon, Lacedaemonia). Southeastern region of the Peloponessus, encompassing within its borders the city of Sparta.

Lē′.thē. The river of oblivion or forgetfulness, situated in the underworld.

Lē′.tō (Latona). Mother of Apollo and Artemis, by Zeus.

Limn, v. Depict; draw or paint.

Man′.u.mit′.ted, pa.ppl. Liberated from bondage.

Mas.sy, adj. Solid and weighty.

Me.du′.sa. A Gorgon (q.v.).

Nec.tar. Drink of the gods.

Nī′.kē. Goddess of victory, usually represented as winged.

O.bol. Ancient Greek coin of small worth.

Oe′.a.grus. Father of Orpheus by the nymph Calliope.

Os.sa. A mountain in northern Greece. In their futile attempt to depose the Olympian gods, the giants undertook to pile Mount Ossa upon Mount Pelion.

Pae.on. A hymn of praise or thanksgiving.

Pāles, v. Makes pale.

Par.cae. The Fates (q.v.).

Passion. The suffering of pain or affliction (as in Orpheus' first speech in Act III); also, any strong emotion, especially anger.

Pe.las'.gic, adj. Pelasgian; pertaining to the Pelasgi, pre-Hellenic inhabitants of Greece.

Pē'.li.on. A mountain in northern Greece. See *Ossa*.

Perforce, adv. Compulsorily.

Phil'.o.mel. The nightingale. An Athenian princess raped and deprived of her tongue by her brother-in-law Tereus and, according to Ovid, subsequently transformed into a nightingale.

Phoebē. Diana or Artemis (q.v.); the moon.

Phoebus. Apollo (q.v.); the sun.

Pī.er'.i.a. The birthplace of the muses and of Orpheus, situated in northern Greece. The poets variously refer to the region as Thrace, Pieria, and Dolopia; however, Thrace of the Classical period was situated farther north.

Pī.rē'.nē. Mourning the death of her son, Cenchrius, who had been killed by Artemis, she wept until she was changed into a fountain.

Plaint, sb. Lamentation; complaint.

Pō.sei'.don (Neptune). God of the sea; son of Cronus and brother of Zeus and Hades.

Prē'.scient, adj. Having foreknowledge.

Prō.pon'.tis. The Sea of Marmora, situated between the Black (Euxine) Sea and the Aegean Sea.

Prō'.tē.an (or Prō'.tean), adj. From *Proteus,* a god who could at will assume any form.

Quick, sb. The living.

Rack, sb. Stratospheric clouds, broken and wind-driven.

Rated, v. Berated; chided.

Re'.crē.ant, adj. Faithless (in Zeus' last speech to Prometheus, scene iii); also, as sb., traitor.

Reft, pa.ppl. Bereft; robbed.

Regnant, adj. Reigning.

Rudely. With great force or violence (as in Narrator's speech in *The Golden Lyre*, I.ii).

Ruth, sb. Compassion; pity.

Sī'.rens. Three sister nymphs of the sea who, by their seductive music, lured sailors to their death.

Si'.sy.phus. Founder of Corinth, famous for his cunning. For breaking faith with Hades, he was condemned to Tartarus where he is required to roll a huge stone to the summit of a mountain. When he nears the top, the stone rolls down the mountainside. Thus must he ever renew his fruitless and endless toil.

Slough, sb. A mire; state or condition of degredation or despondence.

Sovereign, adj. Supremely efficacious; effectual, as a remedy; also, royal.

Stelled, pa.ppl. Enstarred; formed into a star or stars.

Sty.gian, adj. Pertaining to the river Styx (q.v.).

Styx. Principal river of the underworld, across which the souls of the dead are ferried by Charon. An oath sworn upon its venerated waters is held inviolable, even by the gods.

Sur'.que.dry, sb. Haughty pride; arrogant presumption.

Tae'.na.rus. A promontory in the southeast of Laconia, near Sparta. Taenarus contained a deep cavern regarded as an entrance to the underworld. It was through Taenarus that Orpheus gained access to the underworld.

Tan'.ta.lus. A demigod son of Zeus by a nymph; father of Pelops and Niobe. For a heinous sin he is punished in Tartarus with an insatiable thirst and hunger and confined in a clear pool of water on whose banks an apple tree grows. Whenever he attempts to drink the water, it recedes from his lips, and whenever he reaches out to pluck an apple from the tree, its limbs bend away from him.

Tar'.ta.rus. A region of the underworld where Titans are confined and where the most evil of men are punished.

Temerariously. With temerity; in a foolhardy manner.

Tem'.pē. A valley between Mount Olympus and Mount Ossa, described as the most delightful place on earth.

Ten'.e.brous. Profoundly dark; full of darkness.

Tenor, sb. Character; nature; condition.

Thessalia. Thessaly, a region in the extreme north of Greece.

Thunderer. An epithet of Zeus.

Ti.thē′a. The goddess Earth, also called Tellus or Terra.

Tit′.y.us. A Titan who, for his attempted rape of Leto, was slain by Apollo and Artemis and confined to Tartarus. Vultures perpetually feed upon his entrails, which grow again as soon as they are devoured.

Transfix, v. Lit., pierce through.

Trī′.ton. A god of the sea, son of Poseidon.

Tuscan Sea. The Tyrrhenian Sea.

Wherefor, rel.adv. For which; for which reason.

Wherefore, int.adv. Why.

Worm, sb. Serpent.